THE CURSE OF PARTY

The Curse of Party

SWIFT'S RELATIONS WITH

ADDISON AND STEELE

by

Bertrand A. Goldgar

UNIVERSITY OF NEBRASKA PRESS

LINCOLN : 1961

The publication of this book was assisted by
a grant from the Ford Foundation.

To Corinne

PREFACE

It is a commonplace that in the early eighteenth century literature and politics were not the distinct worlds they have since become. In fact, it is difficult to think of a writer of any significance in Queen Anne's England whose life and work were not touched by politics, in even the narrowest sense of that term. And certainly the examples most often cited are those of Swift, Addison, and Steele, whose close friendship was destroyed by what Swift called "this damned business of party." Swift's quarrel with the two Whig essayists is rightly taken as symptomatic of that aspect of the Augustan age which put the most talented writers, even one like Pope who wished to remain neutral, in the center of political conflict. The literary world in 1714 was split along party lines, and no poet or essayist could afford the kind of detachment from politics to which we have grown accustomed in many writers today. Nor was their political commitment merely a matter of party allegiance. Swift and Steele turned their literary talents into political weapons, with each serving as the leading propagandist of his party; and some of Swift's finest political satire grows directly out of his role as Steele's journalistic opponent.

My purpose in this study is to examine in some detail the personal, political, and literary relations of these three men, and to set the known facts about their friendship and their quarrels against the background of party warfare and political journalism in the last six years of Queen Anne. Throughout, my emphasis is upon Swift, rather than Addison and Steele, and I have analyzed as much of his political writing as has seemed relevant. The split between him and his Whig friends may also, I think, involve more than politics; for running deeper than the political differences separating these figures are differences about fundamental intellectual, moral, and religious issues of their age. For this reason, I have undertaken in the Introduction to provide a framework of contrasting intellectual traditions and literary assumptions, a framework which is perhaps essential for any real understanding of their overt personal difficulties. The remaining chapters will then investigate their more explicit, if no less complicated, clash over political loyalties and convictions.

I am grateful to the Clarendon Press for permission to quote passages from *The Poems of Jonathan Swift, The Journal to Stella, The Letters of Joseph Addison,* and Steele's *The Englishman;* and to G. Bell and Sons for permission to quote from *The Correspondence of Jonathan Swift.* Quotations from *The Prose Works of Jonathan Swift* are made by permission of Sir Basil Blackwell. Between the inception of this study as a dissertation at Princeton University and its present publication, I have received a great deal of help and advice. I wish to extend my particular thanks to Professor Irvin Ehrenpreis of Indiana University, who made valuable suggestions for revision of the original thesis; and to Professors Henry K. Miller, Jr., of Princeton and Paul A. Olson of the University of Nebraska, for their personal assistance and scholarly advice. I am indebted to the Research Council of Lawrence College for grants which enabled me to continue the project. My greatest thanks, however, are to Professor Louis A. Landa of Princeton, who suggested the subject, supervised the dissertation, and generously provided guidance and encouragement.

CONTENTS

THE CURSE OF PARTY

INTRODUCTION:
INTELLECTUAL DIFFERENCES

To Swift's contemporaries the most significant aspect of his relations with Addison and Steele was his bitter quarrel with them over politics. After his so-called "conversion" to the Tories in 1710, Swift's friendship with the two Whig writers was doomed by the "curse of party," as he himself called it. It was in this light that informed persons viewed the matter at the time. In fact, during the heated warfare between the two parties in 1714, this private dispute became a matter of public interest and comment, and Swift's "desertion" of Addison and Steele was taken by the Whigs as a symbol of his general political apostasy. This contemporary emphasis on politics as the core of the difficulty among the three men is both obvious and accurate; the weight of any modern study of their relations must necessarily lie in the area of political opinions and party maneuvers.

Yet it would be a serious oversight to let the matter rest at that. However mawkish we may find his judgment, Thackeray's contrast of Swift's "savage indignation" with Addison's "lonely serenity" and Steele's "natural tears" serves to remind us that the rift in their friendship perhaps has deeper roots than differences of opinion over particular political issues.[1] One is struck, too, by the fact that the friendship of these writers of talent failed to produce literary fruits of any real consequence—a fact which is perhaps only accidental but which may be indicative of differing interests and talents. Is it possible, then, that underlying the surface of their clash over politics are fundamental differences in taste, temperament, and intellectual outlook? The present chapter will explore this possibility, first by taking stock of their literary relations and then by comparing their attitudes toward three significant intellectual issues: the role of experimental science, the question of the benevolist versus the egoistic view of man, and the corollary problem involving a tendency to "soften" the doctrine of original sin. These areas of comparison are far from exhaustive, but they will serve at least to provide a context of contrasting intellectual and literary traditions. Within such a context a study of their specific personal and political relations becomes more meaningful, and their underlying differences emerge as symptomatic of basic trends in the morality of the age.

1.

For two years before Swift's shift of political allegiance in 1710, he was welcomed into a circle of Whig literary figures dominated by Addison and Steele. This was a period of close friendship and frequent association for the three men, and Swift's life in these years has even been described as that of a Whig wit. We might therefore expect that the literary productions of the "triumvirate"—it is Swift's own term—would give evidence of a set of common interests, of a community of taste. But in both extent and character the literary connections among the three friends fall surprisingly short of anything approaching "collaboration." Though each of the works will be given detailed consideration in subsequent chapters, it is worth taking a brief survey at this point of all the literary points of contact among Swift, Steele, and Addison.

The conversation of Swift and Addison during the early stages of their intimacy must have turned often to literary figures and ideas, but the only evidence of this mutual interest is

Swift's poem *Baucis and Philemon*. Before it was printed, the original version of this poem, which is still extant, was revised on the advice of Addison. Delany reports that Swift was "often wont to mention: that in a poem of not two hundred lines . . . Mr. *Addison* made him blot out fourscore, add fourscore, and alter fourscore." All the revisions suggested by Addison are in the direction of "correctness" and smoothness. The ineffective lines

> One surly Clown lookt out, and said,
> I'll fling the P—pot on your head;
> You sha'n't come here nor get a Sous
> You look like Rogues would rob a House [2]

are entirely deleted. Swift's vigorous contempt for propriety must have seemed merely bad taste to the author of the popular and "correct" *Campaign*.

It is likely that Addison had a hand in revising other poems by Swift in this period, such as *Vanbrug's House,* but the printed version of *Baucis and Philemon* provides the only definite example of the literary fruits of their early friendship. In 1708, however, there appeared the first of the Bickerstaff pamphlets, which are sometimes taken as a collaborative effort on the part of Swift and the Whig wits. Here again the case may easily be overstated. Swift attacked Partridge at least in part because the astrologer had indiscreetly abused the clergy, particularly High Churchmen, and this motive was one which his Whig friends might not have shared.[3] Moreover, Steele's participation in the affair seems to have been limited to occasional sallies in the *Tatler,* though he is occasionally credited with a leading role in the original attack. Swift's Bickerstaff pamphlets, in short, were by no means simply the outgrowth of his friendship with the Whig wits of the coffeehouses.

It appears, too, that Swift's share in the early stages of Steele's *Tatler* was considerably less than has customarily been attributed to him. There are, of course, the famous verses, "A Description of the Morning" and "A Description of a City Shower." But Herbert Davis, in his edition of the *Prose Works,* is able to print only one essay, No. 230, as definitely Swift's and to include only six as possibly his or as containing hints furnished by him. However, he suggests that Swift, without actually contributing many papers, must have had a great deal more to do with the early essays than simply lending Steele the "Bickerstaff" pseudonym.[4] Indeed, Swift was commonly thought to be somehow the "source" or the inspiration of Steele's periodical, if not actually a leading contributor. Thus Sir Andrew Fountaine wrote to Swift in 1710 of "your bastard the 'Tatler,'" and during the heat of his quarrel with Steele in 1713–14 a common motif of Tory propaganda held that *all* of Steele's "wit" came originally from Swift. This was an illusion which Swift was never at any great pains to dispel. It became so firmly established that much later, in 1720, Prior could write him in this vein: "I do not know why you have not buried me as you did Partridge, and given the wits of the age, the Steeles and Addisons, a new occasion of living seven years upon one of your thoughts." [5]

By March, 1711, when the *Spectator* had begun to appear, Swift had already broken with the Whigs and with their leading "wits." As a result he had no share whatever in the undertaking which brought such a measure of fame to Addison and Steele. On one occasion, when a *Spectator* essay (No. 50) made use of one of his "noble hints," he became extremely annoyed. The essay in question described the visit of four Indian kings to England and used the naïveté of the chiefs as a device for satire on manners. "I repent he ever had it," Swift wrote to Stella. "I intended to have written a book on that subject." Except for this one instance of appropriation of an idea originally given Steele for the *Tatler*, there is nothing to connect Swift with the *Spectator*. His comments on the successful enterprise of his former friends varied from generous praise of the essays ("they have all of them had something pretty") to a scornful indictment of the superficiality of their subject matter: "I will not meddle with the Spectator, let him fair-sex it to the world's end." [6]

This, then, is the extent of Swift's literary connections with Addison and Steele: a poem revised with Addison's help; the Bickerstaff pamphlets, undertaken partially as a defense of his Church, not merely as a joke for the amusement of his Whig friends; and two poems, a few essays, and a number of ideas contributed to Steele's *Tatler*. To some degree, this catalogue does reveal a common ground of literary interests; one may point, for example, to Swift's essay on the English language (*Tatler* No. 230), a subject which was further developed by Addison in *Spectator* No. 135 and again by Swift in his *Proposal for Correcting, Improving, and Ascertaining the English Tongue* (1712). And Swift appears to have been at first genuinely sympathetic with the aims of the *Tatler* and with the kind of "wit" which such essays demanded. Despite the political character of his *Examiner,* there are passages in that journal which both in theme and manner sound very much like the essays which Addison and Steele were printing in the *Spectator.* Nevertheless, when one considers both the degree of intimacy among these three writers and their individual talents, the literary results of their having come together at this point in history are not very impressive. The explanation, in part, rests in the diversity of their interests at the moment. Addison and Steele were rising Whig politicians, both of them holders of government posts and only secondarily men of letters. Swift was in England on official ecclesiastical business, and the tracts in support of the Church which he wrote or revised in the years 1708–10 have more biographical significance than the incidental products of his association with the Whig wits. It is possible, too, that certain fundamental differences of temperament or taste may have been responsible for the situation. At any rate, merely on the basis of literary fecundity, Swift as a "Whig man of letters" contrasts markedly with the Swift of the Scriblerus Club, when his genius was given full play in the company of such congenial spirits as Pope, Arbuthnot, and Gay.

2.

We may now consider some of these fundamental differences in temperament or conviction which coincide with the opposing political allegiances of Swift, Addison, and Steele. Though it is difficult to isolate basic "attitudes" from the multitude of factors—personal and emotional, as well as intellectual—which are involved in the convictions of great writers, certain general areas may serve as bases for comparison. One of these is their reaction to what may be loosely termed "experimental science."

Addison's veneration of science is too well known to require comment. "There are none," he writes in *Spectator* No. 420, "who more gratify and enlarge the imagination than the authors of the new philosophy, whether we consider their theories of the earth or heavens, the discoveries they have made by glasses, or any other of their contemplations on nature." [7] Now it is by no means certain that Swift would have disagreed with such a statement. His attitude toward science is characteristically complex. Although his generally humanistic and anti-intellectual habit of mind would prevent him from expressing such enthusiasm, we are not justified in assuming that he contemned all science and scientists per se.[8] On the other hand, as every reader of *A Tale of a Tub* and *Gulliver's Travels* knows, he was quick to attack scientific goals and methods which seemed to him illegitimate; in fact, "projects" and innovations of all sorts and in areas not specifically "scientific" were often satirized by him as the outgrowth of man's pride. Arthur E. Case, commenting on Swift's ridicule of experimentation in Book III of *Gulliver's Travels*, sums the matter up in terms which bring together the political and intellectual themes: "Whiggery, to Swift, is the negation of that certainty which results from adherence to tried and approved procedures." [9]

Of course Addison and Steele engaged occasionally in ridicule of the same abuses of learning which Swift attacked; the account of Sir Nicholas Gimcrack's will in *Tatler* No. 221 is an obvious example of their disparagement of the virtuoso. But the fact remains that Steele himself was a notorious projector, who had dabbled in alchemy and whose schemes ranged from lotteries to "Fish Pools." This aspect of his career was gleefully satirized by his enemies, and even Addison was compelled to laugh at his friend's propensity for projects and innovations.[10] But it was no laughing matter to Steele, who defended projectors as those inspired with "public spirit":

> He in civil life whose thoughts turn upon schemes which may be of general benefit, without further reflection, is called a "projector"; and the man whose mind seems intent upon glorious achievements, a "knight-errant." The ridicule among us runs strong against laudable actions.[11]

An interesting example of a projector encouraged by Addison and Steele and attacked by Swift is William Whiston, a mathema-

tician and divine whose alleged Arianism cost him his professor-
ship at Cambridge in 1710. At the invitation of Addison, Whiston
gave a series of lectures on experimental science and mathematics at Button's coffeehouse, lectures which were given considerable publicity in Steele's periodicals, the *Guardian* and the
Englishman. In his *Memoirs* Whiston expresses his gratitude to
the Whig writers for this favor:

> Upon occasion of the mention of this person, Mr. *Addison*, who
> was excellent every way, as a traveller, as a prose writer, and as a
> poet, who was my particular friend; and who, with his friend Sir
> *Richard Steel*, brought me, upon my banishment from *Cambridge*,
> to have many astronomical lectures at Mr. *Button's* coffee-house,
> near *Covent-Garden*, to the agreeable entertainment of a good num-
> ber of curious persons. . . .[12]

One of Whiston's projects which he pursued with extraordinary
persistence was a method for determining the longitude on sea
and land. This scheme was first announced in the *Guardian* No.
107; and in December of 1713 a letter from Whiston in further
description of the plan was printed in the *Englishman* No. 29,
where Steele took occasion to praise the project as an example
of "the distinct Merit of Speculative and Active Genio's amongst
Men." [13]

Whiston's heterodoxy alone was enough to ensure an attack
by Swift, and in *Mr. Collin's Discourse of Free-Thinking* several
ironic remarks are directed against "poor Mr. *Whiston*, who
denies the Divinity of Christ." But beyond this, Whiston's career
as a projector was certain to bring ridicule from the Scriblerians.
In 1712 Swift had reported to Stella:

> Do you know what the Longitude is? A Projector has been applying
> himself to me to recommend him to the Ministry, because he pre-
> tends to have found out the Longitude. I believe He has no more
> found it out, than he has found out mine _____.[14]

He related this same incident to Archbishop King, in rather more
formal language, with this additional remark: "I understand
nothing of the mathematics; but I am told it is a thing as improbable as the philosopher's stone, or perpetual motion." [15]
This particular projector may have been Whiston, though many
others were seeking to solve the same problem. At any rate,

when the details of Whiston's plan were finally revealed in July of 1714, Arbuthnot wrote to Swift complaining that the absurdity of the actual scheme had spoiled a satire he had intended on that subject:

> Whiston has at last published his project of the longitude; the most ridiculous thing that ever was thought on. But a pox on him! he has spoiled one of my papers of Scriblerus, which was a proposal for the longitude, not very unlike his. . . .

To this the Dean replied, "It was a malicious satire of yours upon Whiston, that what you intended as a ridicule, should be any way struck upon by him for a reality." [16] Swift's contempt for Whiston, as contrasted with Addison's and Steele's generous encouragement, has some political overtones, for the Tories accused the Whigs of sponsoring the eccentric divine when his theological views brought him into difficulty. But perhaps, too, the case of Whiston is indicative of a more fundamental difference in attitude toward the "distinct Merit of Speculative and Active Genio's amongst Men."

3.

These varying reactions of Swift, Addison, and Steele to the "scientific" experiments of a man like Whiston are significant, but far more interesting are their contrasting positions on a matter of even greater importance to their contemporaries: the nature of man. This is a question, really, of basic assumptions rather than overt argument, for Swift and Steele, even when their quarrel is most bitter, seldom attack each other on the grounds of ethical or religious principles. But some writers later in the century made it clear that they recognized in the work of Swift and his friends contrasting views of human nature, views which may have been responsible for the different directions in which their literary talents lay. Thus James Harris has this advice for the reader of *Gulliver's Travels:* "Whoever has been reading this *unnatural* Filth, let him turn for a moment to a *Spectator* of ADDISON, and observe the PHILANTHROPY of that *Classical Writer;* I may add the *superior* Purity of his *Diction* and his *Wit.*" And in his *Conjectures on Original Composition* Edward Young, who had been on very friendly terms with Steele during

1713–14, accuses Swift of having made a monster of the "Human face divine" by his satire on human nature. Addison, he says, "prescribed a wholesome and pleasant regimen, which was universally relished, and did much good"; whereas Swift "insisted on a large dose of ipecacuanha, which, tho' readily swallowed from the fame of the physician, yet, if the patient had any delicacy of taste, he threw up the remedy, instead of the disease." [17]

In the most general terms the contrast suggested by these comments is between the satirist's and the sentimentalist's views of human nature. It is a phenomenon often remarked that in the early eighteenth century these views seem to run parallel to political ideologies. The Tory satirists pessimistically assumed that the evil in the world has its origins in the corruption within man. The Whig literary circles, on the other hand, encouraged a more modern spirit, a more sympathetic view of human nature, and their attitudes underlay the literature of sensibility which gradually prevailed as the century progressed.[18] This generalization fits the case of Swift, Addison, and Steele well enough, but only if we exercise considerable caution. It is neither possible nor desirable to place these writers in separate, distinct "schools" of thought. Though their ethical differences are real, they are often manifested simply as differences in tone or in basic assumptions that are not directly expressed. Rigid categorizing becomes impossible, too, because in this instance the points of conflict were not as obvious as they might have been a few decades later. But it is nonetheless essential to gain some knowledge of the currents of ideas to which Swift, Addison, and Steele were indebted.

For the sake of convenience, we may review this intellectual background in terms of separate strains of thought which in reality are interconnected and overlap. One such element is the whole complex of ideas known as "benevolism." The ethics of benevolence, good nature, and sentimental feeling have been traced to the preaching of Latitudinarian divines of the late seventeenth and early eighteenth centuries. Tillotson, Barrow, South, and others of this tradition identified virtue with acts of benevolence and developed a psychology of "natural goodness" which viewed man as instinctively inclined toward benevolent love of others.[19] In a more systematic way Shaftesbury, Hutcheson, and other moralists of the early part of the eighteenth century, especially those of the so-called "moral sense" school, also set about reconciling virtue and interest. Their method, it may be noted, frequently involved a kind of underlying dualism of the passions: man has within him both a principle of self-love and a principle of natural benevolence.[20] Indeed, the development of such an ethic was paralleled by a general rehabilitation of the passions; within the context of the traditional anti-Stoic and Peripatetic positions there occurred a shift of emphasis from simple toleration of the affections toward a greater confidence in the passions as seeds of virtue, beneficial to man both psychologically and ethically.[21]

In contrast to this benevolist ethic is a more pessimistic tradition which traces all the actions of men to a basic egoism. Thus La Rochefoucauld's maxims emphasize continually the pervasiveness of self-love as a determining force of all our actions. Man is a creature deceived by the force of his passions, and "Les passions ne sont que les divers gouts de l'amour-propre." Such a doctrine, in La Rochefoucauld and others, was often accompanied by a psychological antirationalism: self-love and the derivative passions are more powerful than reason.[22] The same cynical reduction of human acts and motives to a fundamental self-love is at the heart of both Hobbes and Mandeville, in different contexts; and Christian moralists, especially those of a Calvinistic tendency, accept this view of human nature as a demonstration of man's depravity. R. S. Crane points out that when the Latitudinarian divines depicted benevolent feelings as natural to man, they were reacting both against Hobbes and against the Puritan insistence on man's corrupt state.[23]

In Swift's day, then, there were two basic lines of moral thought which must be taken into account in a comparison of his ideas with those of his Whig friends. Actually, the principles of "benevolism" seldom appear in the essays of Addison and Steele in any very explicit form. A decade later these ideas were much more firmly embodied in the writings of popular moralists than they were in 1712. For example, the *Hibernicus's Letters* (1725–26) of James Arbuckle, who greatly admired Addison, contains numerous passages in this vein:

My Readers will remember, that in a former Paper, I endeavoured to shew, that *Nature* having implanted in us a Principle of *Benevolence,* the *Pursuits* of it must necessarily be attended with great and real *Pleasure.* . . . I now proceed to illustrate farther this Subject, by giving Instances of some of those *Joyful* Effects, which *Benevolence* has upon those generous Minds that are animated by it.[24]

In an ironic letter of complaint Arbuckle accused himself of having been too greatly influenced by Shaftesbury, the *Spectator,* Hutcheson, Wollaston, "and such other dull *Rationalists.*" Actually, the *Spectator* contains no such overt formulations of the benevolist doctrines except for two essays in the eighth volume by Henry Grove, Nos. 588 and 601. Nevertheless, Addison and, especially, Steele do on occasion betray very definite inclinations in this direction.

It is in his early work *The Christian Hero,* rather than in the *Tatler* or *Spectator,* that Steele speaks most directly about such matters. Miss Rae Blanchard, in her analysis of this attack on the "meer morality" of the Stoics, indicates that Steele did accept in part the egoistic, antirationalistic theory that man is dominated by selfish passions. But he refused, she says, to draw completely pessimistic conclusions from such a view. Side by side with these signs of depravity he found in man a natural "temper of mind" which encourages virtue; men are "framed for mutual Kindness" by the "Force of their Make."[25] He expresses confidence in the passions as springs of action and optimistically depicts human nature as naturally inclined toward benevolence.

Though this general point of view in *The Christian Hero* may underlie the obvious sentimentality of all the rest of Steele's work—in the plays, for instance—its appearances in any systematic or explicit form are curiously infrequent. Only occasionally does his writing exposit directly this current of ideas. In the dedication of the *Lover* to Garth he praises that elusive concept "good nature" as the worthiest affection of the mind because it "diffuses its Benevolence to all the World." And in the *Spectator* (No. 230) he contrasts the view of human nature which shows us as "deformed" and evil with the view which reveals men as "mild, good, and benevolent, full of a generous regard for the public prosperity, compassionating each other's

distresses and relieving each other's wants. . . ." Again, in the
unlikely context of a bitter political tract (*The Importance of
Dunkirk*), Steele takes occasion to praise the "social Virtues"
such as benevolence to mankind in an effort to show that he
himself has been animated by this "Charity" in his political
writings. Apparently even when "benevolence" is adapted to
political purposes, it will be accompanied by a "self-approving
joy": "He who has warm'd his Heart with Impressions of this
kind, will find Glowings of Good-will, which will support him
in the Service of his Country. . . ." [26] Finally, it may be noted
that when Steele does directly discuss these concepts his remarks
are not always entirely consistent. Thus *Spectator* No. 280 praises
actions done from "innate benevolence" rather than "vanity
to excel," whereas in a later essay, No. 356, Steele states the orthodox view that future rewards and punishments are the most
noble incentive to worthy actions—we are simply flattering ourselves if we believe that we can act from motives which are
"wholly disinterested" or if we find ourselves "divested of any
views arising from self-love and vainglory."

No matter how infrequent or how inconsistent Steele's comments on benevolism may be, some of his contemporaries apparently felt that he represented a benevolist point of view.
It may or may not be of any importance that a sermon by Francis
Squire entitled *Universal Benevolence: or, Charity in its Full
Extent* (1714) should have been "humbly dedicated to Richard
Steele." [27] But it is undoubtedly significant that Mandeville
himself should single out Steele for attack, in a passage which
ironically suggests that Steele's flattery of man is only a cynical
trick:

> When the Incomparable Sir *Richard Steele,* in the usual Elegance
> of his easy Style, dwells on the Praises of his sublime Species, and
> with all the Embellishments of Rhetoric sets forth the Excellency
> of Human Nature, it is impossible not to be charm'd with his happy
> Turns of Thought, and the Politeness of his Expressions. But tho'
> I have been often moved by the Force of his Eloquence, and ready
> to swallow the ingenious Sophistry with Pleasure, yet I could never
> be so serious, but reflecting on his artful Encomiums I thought on
> the Tricks made use of by Women that would teach Children to be
> mannerly.[28]

Mandeville might have included Addison, too, in his ridicule; in fact Hutcheson, when attacking the *Fable of the Bees,* mentions Addison as one of the "Men of Reflection" who have taught that our chief pleasure in life consists in love of God and in kind affections to our fellow creatures.[29] But in Addison, as in Steele, the benevolist ethic is more often implicit than directly stated. Like Steele and many other traditional Christian moralists, he attacks the Stoics, whose "wise man" cannot even feel pity for the afflictions of others; the Christian compassion which they deny themselves is "a kind of pleasing anguish, as well as generous sympathy, that knits mankind together, and blends them in the same common lot." Self-love, Addison admits, is an instinct placed in us for our own good, but in the same way we are also provided with other, more benevolent instincts: love of our families, love of our country, and the benevolence due to all mankind. He speaks, too, of the inward delight and secret pleasure which the virtuous man feels in doing good, and he defines charity as "a habit of good-will, or benevolence, in the soul, which disposes us to the love, assistance, and relief of mankind, especially of those who stand in need of it." [30]

This "habit" in the soul is apparently what Addison means by "good nature," which he analyzes in more detail than he does the other aspects of benevolist thought. Good nature is an innate characteristic and an ornament to virtue which enables us to extinguish much of the misery of life by "mutual offices of compassion, benevolence, and humanity." But Addison further distinguishes good nature as an inherent trait from good nature as a moral virtue. To determine whether or not our instinctive good nature is a moral virtue, we may measure it against certain criteria: it must be steady and uniform; it must operate according to the rules of reason, making distinctions between deserving and undeserving objects; and it must be an impulse powerful enough to make us willing to risk our fortune and reputation for the benefit of all men.[31]

On the basis of his analysis of good nature as a "moral virtue," it might be possible to align Addison with some particular "school" of benevolism; but it seems to me that neither he nor Steele discusses these concepts at sufficient length or with sufficient directness to make such distinctions meaningful in their case. They lean heavily toward the benevolist view of man, as the comments cited above clearly indicate, but except for *The Christian Hero,* Steele and Addison were writing essays, not tracts, and such moral theories would appear more as assumptions and general tendencies than as clearly formulated ethical systems. But these assumptions should now be clear. Maynard Mack has described Pope's *Essay on Man* as an effort to steer between the egoist theory of Hobbes and Mandeville on one side and the benevolist theories of Shaftesbury and Hutcheson on the other.[32] However incomplete their formal statements on the subject may be, it is obvious that the same thing could not be said of Addison and Steele.

Nor was Swift inclined to steer a middle course between these extremes. His ethic rests on the assumption that man is dominated by self-love and the selfish passions; those who feel that man can create his own standards, or can determine for himself matters of right and wrong, are ignoring the limitations of human reason and the corrupt state of human nature. Instead, morality must be based on a conscience which uses standards originating outside of man's limited world. Such a conscience prompts man to virtuous conduct by appealing to his selfish nature; and "enlightened" self-interest encourages him to act virtuously in the hope of an eternal reward.[33]

Thus in his sermon *On the Testimony of Conscience,* which Professor Landa suggests may be an oblique answer to Shaftesbury, Swift expresses his conviction that corrupt man can achieve virtue only through the guidance of a conscience which keeps him in mind of future rewards and punishments. It is only a conscience founded on religion which can ensure proper conduct, "since there is no other Tie thro' which the Pride, or Lust, or Avarice, or Ambition of Mankind will not certainly break one Time or other." [34] With the same cynicism Swift goes on to attack the "meer moral Man" whose morality is purely secular; if examined, his "virtuous" conduct proves to be little more than an indulgence of his own ease and interest. The same ideas appear in his anti-Stoic sermon *Upon the Excellency of Christianity,* which thus forms an interesting contrast to Steele's anti-Stoic tract *The Christian Hero.* Here again Swift shows that only Christianity takes a "realistic" view of man as a selfish

creature because only Christianity involves the doctrine of future judgment. Man can be induced to live virtuously only by
an appeal to his higher self-interest, his hope for eternal reward:

> Now, human nature is so constituted, that we can never pursue any
> thing heartily but upon hopes of a reward. If we run a race, it is
> in expectation of a prize, and the greater the prize the faster we
> run; for an incorruptible crown, if we understand it and believe it
> to be such, more than a corruptible one. But some of the philos-
> ophers gave all this quite another turn, and pretended to refine so
> far, as to call virtue its own reward, and worthy to be followed only
> for itself. . . .[35]

Obviously there is little place in such an ethical system for a
concept of natural benevolence or "good nature." Addison, it
will be recalled, had defined "charity" as a habit of benevolence
in the soul which disposes us to love one another. Swift's sermon
On Mutual Subjection, basically a conventional charity sermon,
ignores the benevolist doctrine which was prevalent in many
such sermons. In his introduction to the sermons Professor Landa
reminds us that Swift's cynical view of man, so obvious in his
other work, would not permit him in this sermon to identify
charity as the product of a benevolence naturally rooted in men.
He shows, too, that Swift avoids dwelling in detail on the "inward delight" of doing good, a subject which was customarily a
part of such sermons and which Addison elaborated in Spectator
No. 257. Similarly, it is unlikely that Addison or Steele would
have felt sympathetic to the attitude expressed in the opening
passage of Swift's sermon Doing Good:

> Nature directs every one of us, and God permits us, to consult our
> own private Good before the private Good of any other person
> whatsoever. We are, indeed, commanded to love our Neighbour as
> ourselves, but not as well as ourselves. . . . And this I need not be
> at much pains in persuading you to; for the want of self-love, with
> regard to things of this world, is not among the faults of mankind.[36]

Swift's view of man, then, has closer affinities with the "egoistic" school of La Rochefoucauld, Hobbes, and Mandeville
than with the benevolist line of thought to which Addison and
Steele are often indebted. Oddly enough, the basic difference
in their points of view was made clear in one of Swift's tracts

written while he and Steele were still on cordial terms: *A Project for the Advancement of Religion and the Reformation of Manners,* published in 1709. As will be shown in the following chapter, this tract, though it received high praise from Steele, actually takes a position much unlike his; for Swift here bases his proposals for reform on the assumption that all men are dominated by self-love and that only a plan for reformation which is founded realistically on man's selfishness can hope to succeed.

In 1714, five years after the publication of the *Project,* the quarrel between Swift and Steele was at its height. It is of some significance, I think, that the principal attack on Swift by a defender of Steele should have utilized the "intellectual" as well as political differences between them. Underlying this entire satire, entitled *Essays Divine, Moral and Political,* is an effort to place Swift in a Mandevillian or egoistic school of moralists and to apply the *reductio* method to these ethical assumptions. The central device is for "Swift," as the supposed author of the essays, to expound a distorted version of the doctrine that self-interest is the root of all behavior and to explain how this principle has guided his own conduct. Thus the essay on "Virtue" explains that this term is meaningless, since all human activity proceeds from vanity or ambition; and the essay entitled "Friendship" justifies Swift's treatment of Steele on the ground that self-love must govern in such a relationship as in everything else. Moreover, "wit" is depicted as hostile to Christianity, and "satire" is taken as the opposite of "charity." The authorship of this volume is uncertain; but by adopting the point of view of both a Whig and a benevolist, the writer, whoever he may have been, has very adroitly set the political and personal differences between Steele and Swift in a wider framework of opposing ethical ideas.

4.

The two lines of thought which have been examined thus far are directly related to another question of extreme interest to Swift and his contemporaries: the doctrine of original sin and the concept of natural depravity. During the first few decades of the century a climate of opinion had been established which was decidedly hostile to the traditional interpretation of the Fall of Man. In a sense the optimistic view of human nature implicit in the teachings of the benevolists is one element in a revival of the Pelagian heresy on both a secular and theological level in the late seventeenth and early eighteenth centuries. And one reflection of this on the literary scene was an increasing attack on "general" satire as an insult to the "dignity of human nature." [37]

A study of the manner in which the doctrine of natural depravity became "softened" is beyond the scope of this chapter, but a few examples of the reaction may be cited from moralists of the late seventeenth century. To some degree, the tendency to discount the effects of the Fall on human nature cuts across different schools of thought. All those who wished to contravert either the Calvinistic insistence on man's corrupt state or the cynicism of Hobbes and Mandeville, or both, were led in this direction. Thus the Stoic Antoine Le Grand can write:

> It must be owned that human nature is not so depraved as they describe her, that she yet retains some of her purity, and that man hath still a power to combat vice, follow vertue, and conquer his *Passions*.[38]

At the same time, anti-Stoic moralists intent on rehabilitating the passions may ring changes on the same theme. James Lowde, in *A Discourse Concerning the Nature of Man* (1694), attacks the Stoics and defends the passions as seeds of virtue, but his toleration of the inferior faculties rests on an assumption of "natural goodness" similar to Le Grand's. Another moralist, Timothy Nourse, carries this chain of thought to its logical extreme and reaches a remarkable conclusion: because of the passions, "Man at present is a more Excellent Creature than he was in the State of Innocence." [39] Of course, much more important than these moralists in propagating the doctrines of innate goodness were the Latitudinarian divines. Like Nourse and Lowde, they would agree with Le Grand's optimistic view, but for completely different purposes and in a context of Christian benevolism. R. S. Crane has pointed out that when divines such as Barrow, Tillotson, or South depicted benevolent feelings as natural to man, they were reacting not only against Hobbes but also against the Puritan insistence on natural depravity.[40]

In the eighteenth century these ideas gathered force, so that by the end of the century we find William Wilberforce complaining that the generality of professed Christians either completely ignore or greatly extenuate the doctrine of natural corruption, which is the basis of Christianity. Most people, he says, consider man as a being naturally pure and inclined to virtue. "Vice with them is rather an accidental and temporary, than a constitutional and habitual distemper. . . . Far different is the humiliating language of Christianity." [41] Even in the first half of the century the explicit denial of original sin was sufficiently prevalent in moral and religious writing to provoke a certain amount of formal theological controversy. Though much of this controversy occurred somewhat later than the period with which we are immediately concerned, some brief mention of the dispute will be of value. It will, at least, give evidence that before the death of Swift and only a decade after the death of Steele it was necessary to defend the doctrine of original sin against open and widespread attack.

Around 1740 John Taylor of Norwich gave a fully developed statement of the new Pelagianism in his influential work, *The Scripture-Doctrine of Original Sin.* Taylor agrees that the sin of Adam has resulted in our sorrow, labor, and mortality, but he insists that our faith in this article of religion need extend no farther. We are born not in sin but in ignorance; and our passions and appetites, though they may become evil through excess or abuse, are in themselves good. He protests against those who consider only the imperfection of man: "To disparage our Nature, is to disparage the Work and Gifts of God." [42] Taylor was answered by a number of divines, including John Wesley, Samuel Hebden, Isaac Watts, and Jonathan Edwards.[43] All of them point to the doctrine of original sin as the "foundation" of Christianity, since to deny that man is sinful by nature is to obviate the doctrine of the Redemption and divine grace. Significantly, too, some of them indirectly defend satirists who "disparage our Nature" by pointing to their satires as *evidence* that man is corrupt. Wesley, as T. O. Wedel has pointed out, quotes sections of the fourth part of *Gulliver's Travels* and describes Swift's passages as no more than the "naked truth." "And meanwhile," he adds sarcastically, "we gravely talk of the 'dignity of our nature' in its present state!" [44] Watts, too, in his *Ruin and Recovery of Mankind* (1740), speaks of man's degeneracy as the subject of satire:

> Should the Poets or Philosophers form a just Idea of it, as far as our common Capacities extend, there would be criminal and absurd Matter enough to furnish a *Horace* or a *Juvenal* with a thousand Jests and Sarcasms on their own Species, or rather with a thousand full Satires.[45]

Wesley describes Taylor's volume as only one manifestation of a "deadly poison which has been diffusing itself for several years through our nation, our Church, and even our Universities." The influence of Shaftesbury and other benevolist writers in spreading this "poison" has already been mentioned. One other source from which it emanated was the deists, for their rational systems naturally had no place for the traditional ideas of original sin and natural depravity. Thus Matthew Tindal's *Christianity as old as the Creation* (1730) complains that these doctrines constitute a "Libel on the Dignity of Human Nature; and an high Reflection on the Wisdom and Goodness of its Author." In answer to his argument, John Leland contents himself with the fact that "innate Pravity" of human nature has been recognized by historians, poets, philosophers, and politicians in all ages, and John Balguy answers Tindal with the same appeal to the evidence of history and literature.[46]

Finally, a summary indictment of those members of the English clergy who deny original sin appears in Robert Wightman's preface to *Human Nature in its Fourfold State,* a popular work by the Scotch Presbyterian Thomas Boston. In this preface, added in 1729, Wightman finds it remarkable that so obvious and important a truth as the depravity of human nature should be misunderstood or doubted by any who call themselves ministers:

> Are there not persons to be found in a neighbouring nation, in the character of preachers, appearing daily in pulpits who are so unacquainted with their Bibles and themselves, that they ridicule the doctrine of Original sin as unintelligible jargon? . . . These are the men who talk of the dignity of human nature, of greatness of mind, nobleness of soul, and generosity of spirit: as if they intended to

persuade themselves and others, that pride is a good principle, and do not know, that pride and selfishness are the bane of mankind productive of all the wickedness, and much of the misery to be found in this and in the other world, and is indeed that, wherein the depravity of human nature properly consists.[47]

It will be noted that Wightman and some of the other writers cited above use the phrase "the dignity of human nature" to represent the entire line of thought which viewed man as naturally good and as unaffected by the consequences of original sin. In the essays or tracts of secular moralists, the same phrase often becomes the shibboleth which indicates each writer's attitude toward such questions, even though he may not discuss them in explicitly theological terms. Hume's essay "Of the Dignity or Meanness of Human Nature" describes the division in the "learned world" on just this point:

> Some exalt our species to the skies, and represent man as a kind of human demigod, who derives his origin from heaven, and retains evident marks of his lineage and descent. Others insist upon the blind sides of human nature, and can discover nothing, except vanity, in which man surpasses the other animals, whom he affects so much to despise. If an author possess the talent of rhetoric and declamation, he commonly takes part with the former: If his turn lie towards irony and ridicule, he naturally throws himself into the other extreme.[48]

Hume goes on to suggest that the favorable view of man is more conducive to virtue and to align himself with those who believe that social passions predominate over unselfish principles in our nature. His own views, however, need not concern us. The significant aspect of the essay is his exposition of the opposing attitudes toward the dignity of human nature and his identification of satiric talent with the "pessimistic" view of man. Satires "on man" were, of course, a well-established tradition, and the theme of theriophily, which Hume touches upon, was often used as a weapon to attack man's pride in his supposed dignity.[49]

As we have seen, the increasing tendency in the early eighteenth century to deny original sin, either tacitly or directly, and to paint man as naturally prone to virtue, created an atmosphere quite hostile to such "general" satire. The benevolist Arbuckle ridicules those moralists who debase human nature while they attempt to correct it; for man cannot possibly be reformed if "the whole Frame has been originally wicked and perverse; which certainly is the Supposition of those Gentlemen who make Self-Love the Source and Center of all human Actions." [50] As might be expected, he also attacks satirists who draw an unfavorable picture of human nature. Discourses on mankind, he says, will be either wholly satire or panegyric, and the determining factor is always the character of the writer. A few men are even led so far by their spleen and their folly that they depict some of the brute species as a more excellent kind of being than mankind. In his essay for February 26, 1725/6, only a few months before the publication of *Gulliver's Travels*, Arbuckle indicts as "common enemies" of man all those who represent us as naturally selfish and propagate notions derogatory to our species:

> Several grave Divines, out of an intemperate Zeal for the Honour of Religion, from a misapplication of several Passages in Scripture, have taken upon them to represent Human Nature in such a manner, that if we really believed what they say, we should think ourselves but little obliged to our Creator for the Being he has bestowed upon us. . . .
>
> I am confident, that were there any Species of Brutes endued with the Faculty of Speech, they could not load the Human Nature with more opprobrious Epithets, than has been done by some who have had the Honour to wear it.[51]

In the same way John Hughes, writing much earlier in the *Spectator,* had complained that satirists who "describe nothing but deformity" are only mistaking spleen for philosophy: " 'It is very disingenuous to level the best of mankind with the worst, and for the faults of particulars to degrade the whole species.' " [52] But it is hardly surprising that writers whose underlying assumptions caused them to question the doctrine of natural depravity and to champion the "dignity of human nature" should have little taste for what the eighteenth century called "levelling" satire.

Enough has been said already of Swift's ethics to make obvious his reaction to this related question of original sin. His insistence on our "corrupt nature" and his rejection of any system which assumes that man has a natural capacity for virtue are inseparable from his conviction of the reality of the Fall. As a result of his "intemperate Zeal for the Honour of Religion," to use Arbuckle's phrase, he condemned the contemporary tendency toward Pelagianism. The point need not be elaborated here, but it should be noted that recent interpretations of *Gulliver's Travels,* especially Part Four, emphasize the role which such convictions play in that satire.[53] Wesley, it is now realized, had correctly interpreted Swift's satire as a polemic against those who praise the dignity of human nature, deny original sin, and thus subvert the doctrine of the Redemption. Professor Roland Frye, in fact, has shown that Swift's portrayal of the Yahoos employs the symbols and metaphors commonly used by theologians to depict human sin and corruption. As a clergyman Swift considered the problem of human nature in terms of orthodox Christianity—and orthodox Christianity reminds man that he is a fallen creature in need of grace, naturally prone to sin and not to virtue. *Gulliver's Travels,* as a great work of art, obviously involves much more than this; but we seriously misunderstand Swift's satire if we fail to relate it to this contemporary background. Both as a "general" satire and as a delineation of man in his corrupt state, *Gulliver's Travels* firmly aligns Swift against those like Arbuckle who sentimentalized human nature and impugned the efficacy of original sin.

The attitudes of Addison and Steele toward these questions are less easy to come by. Once again, the difference between their point of view and Swift's is often a matter of tone and is revealed only occasionally in their writings. Certainly, neither ever directly attacks the doctrine of original sin; they were popular essayists, not clergymen or theologians. But some of their remarks, when viewed in the light of the controversy I have surveyed, are revealing. Thus Steele can praise the "dignity of human nature" in this way:

> There is nothing which I contemplate with greater pleasure than the dignity of human nature, which often shows itself in all conditions of life; for notwithstanding the degeneracy and meanness that is crept into it, there are a thousand occasions in which it breaks through its original corruption, and shows what it once was, and what it will be hereafter. I consider the soul of man as the ruin of a glorious pile of building; where, amidst great heaps of rubbish, you meet with noble fragments of sculpture, broken pillars and obelisks, and a magnificence in confusion.[54]

Addison, too, expresses pleasure in the natural dignity of man, which in his view is demonstrated by man's faculty of reason.[55] And perhaps both Addison and Steele are in Hume's mind when he writes that "all our polite and fashionable moralists" insist upon a favorable view of mankind as more advantageous to virtue.

Hume, it will be recalled, contrasts such "moralists" with those whose talent lies in the direction of irony and ridicule and who consequently are led to "depreciate" our species. There is much in the attitude of Addison and Steele toward satire itself which reveals their distaste for that "group" which insists upon exposing the frailties of human nature. Steele, for example, believes that "good-nature" and a "benevolence to all men" are essential qualities of the satirist, and Addison finds that even the best personal satire is the product of an evil mind. He writes, "I once had gone through half a satire, but found so many motions of humanity rising in me towards the persons whom I had severely treated, that I threw it into the fire without ever finishing it." [56] The contrast between good nature and humanity, on the one hand, and "wit," raillery, and satire, on the other, is a recurrent motif in the *Spectator*.

Of course, for Addison to deplore personal satire and lampoons is not surprising or particularly significant; such protests were common enough. But elsewhere he makes it clear that the whole satiric temper of mind is alien to him. He resolves to publish only essays which are written in the spirit of benevolence and love of man, and the reception of the *Spectator* convinces him that "the world is not so corrupt as we are apt to imagine; and that if those men of parts who have been employed in vitiating the age had endeavoured to rectify and amend it, they needed not have sacrificed their good sense and virtue to their fame and reputation." [57] It is especially significant that Addison, like Hughes and Arbuckle, should attack "general" satire as an insult to the dignity of human nature:

I must confess, there is nothing that more pleases me in all that I read in books, or see among mankind, than such passages as represent human nature in its proper dignity. As man is a creature made up of different extremes, he has something in him very great and very mean: a skilful artist may draw an excellent picture of him

in either of these views. The finest authors of antiquity have taken
him on the more advantageous side. . . . On the contrary, I could
never read any of our modish French authors, or those of our own
country who are the imitators and admirers of that trifling nation,
without being for some time out of humour with myself, and at
everything about me. Their business is to depreciate human nature,
and consider it under its worst appearances. They give mean interpretations and base motives to the worthiest actions; they resolve
virtue and vice into constitution. In short, they endeavour to make
no distinction between man and man, or between the species of
men and that of brutes.[58]

As an instance of this kind of author, he cites La Rochefoucauld,
whom Swift termed his "favorite." Similarly, in *Spectator* No.
209, Addison takes occasion to attack the satire of Juvenal and
Boileau:

Such levelling satires are of no use to the world, and for this reason
I have often wondered how the French author above mentioned,
who was a man of exquisite judgment, and a lover of virtue, could
think human nature a proper subject for satire in another of his
celebrated pieces, which is called 'The Satire upon Man.' What
vice or frailty can a discourse correct which censures the whole
species alike, and endeavours to show by some superficial strokes of
wit, that brutes are the more excellent creatures of the two? A satire
should expose nothing but what is corrigible, and make a due dis-
crimination between those who are, and those who are not, the
proper objects of it.[59]

Such a comment demonstrates strikingly, I think, the temperamental and intellectual differences between Addison and the
author of *Gulliver's Travels*.

It is true, however, that in other contexts Addison occasionally
approaches Swift in his condemnation of man's pride and his
references to human depravity. But even here the tone is far from
Swift's. Consider, for example, this passage from *Guardian* No.
153, in which Addison ridicules human vanity through the device of a molehill inhabited by rational pismires:

If now you have a mind to see all the ladies of the mole-hill, observe
first the pismire that listens to the emmet on her left hand, at the
same time that she seems to turn away her head from him. He tells
this poor insect that she is a goddess, that her eyes are brighter than

the sun, that life and death are at her disposal. She believes him, and gives herself a thousand little airs upon it. Mark the vanity of the pismire on your left hand. She can scarcely crawl with age; but you must know she values herself upon her birth; and if you mind, spurns at every one that comes within her reach. The little nimble coquette that is running along by the side of her, is a wit. She has broke many a pismire's heart. Do but observe what a drove of lovers are running after her.[60]

Here both the subject of the satire and the satiric device are similar to Swift's, but the tone and attitude are those not of *Gulliver's Travels* but of the *Spectator,* and especially of that strain in the *Spectator* which caused Swift to remark, "Let him fair-sex it till the world's end." Even when Addison chooses to remind us of the meanness and not the dignity of human nature, he does so without the indignation which Hume singles out as characteristic of the satiric view of human nature and which we normally associate with Swift. Instead we find, in Steele's words, "that smiling mirth, that delicate satire, and genteel raillery, which appeared in Mr. Addison when he was free among his intimates." [61]

Swift, Addison, and Steele cannot, then, be placed in rigidly distinct categories in regard to such questions as experimental science and the nature of man. Yet analysis does reveal very significant differences of tone, of temperament, and of underlying assumptions which are not overtly expressed. An examination of the complex of ideas which informed the minds of their contemporaries throws these differences into relief and does much to explain the ease with which Harris and Young could prescribe the "philanthropy" of Addison as an antidote to the satire of Swift. The chapters which follow are concerned primarily with the political and personal relations between these three writers; they deal, in other words, with all that is external and explicit in their relationship. But, to state it once again, it is perhaps in the context of contrasting literary and intellectual traditions that these more obvious aspects of their relations can be best understood.

I

SWIFT IN ENGLAND,
1707-1709

FROM November of 1707 until June of 1709 Swift resided in England, the purpose of his visit being to secure the remission of those taxes on the Irish clergy known as the First Fruits and Twentieth Parts. This was a period of his life marked by a succession of expectations and disappointments in the accomplishment of his "official" mission and in his hopes for his own preferment. At this time, too, he was admitted into that circle of poets and politicians whom he was later to call the "Whig wits." These are the years of his closest friendship with Addison and Steele, and it is with this aspect of his visit that the present chapter is primarily concerned.

We must not, however, place too much emphasis on Swift's association with this group of friends or, as is sometimes done, view him during this visit to England as a Whig man of letters. If this was the time of intimacy with Addison, Steele, and Philips, and of friendship with such "great men" among the Whigs as Somers, Sunderland, and Halifax, it was also a time when Swift became increasingly disillusioned with the Godolphin ministry on two counts affecting the Church: their failure to secure a grant remitting the First Fruits and their efforts to repeal the Sacramental Test clause. The writings which are sometimes thought of as the fruit of Swift's association with the Whig wits, such as the Bickerstaff papers and the contributions to the *Tatler*, are less important biographically than the tracts in support of the Church of England which he wrote or revised in 1708 and which he later adduced, after his alignment with the Tories, as evidence of his political consistency. His shift of political allegiance in 1710 has its roots at least as far back as this earlier visit to England, and to the extent that political differences are responsible for the rupture of his friendship with Addison and Steele, it may be said that the break was beginning at the very time when the friendship seemed most strong.

We must realize also that at no time in these two years did Swift become as deeply committed to a political party as were Addison and Steele. Both, when he met them, were well entrenched as Whig "party-men" and as members of the Kit-Kat Club; and both held government posts, Steele as the Gazetteer and Addison as the Undersecretary for Sunderland, the senior Secretary of State. Addison had inaugurated his political career in 1705 with the publication of the *Campaign,* and now in 1708, the initial year of his friendship with Swift, he issued anonymously a phamphlet which illustrates his thorough support of government policy. *The Present State of the War, and the Necessity of an Augmentation, Considered* takes as a major premise that *"no peace is to be made without an entire disunion of the* French *and* Spanish *Monarchies,"* a "fixt Rule" which was to form the core of the Whig opposition to the Peace of Utrecht.[1]

From the outset, then, Swift's interests were somewhat different from those of his new friends, whose principles and personal ambitions were firmly attached to the Whig cause. Neither his friendship with the "great men" of the Junto nor his association with the Whig wits of the coffeehouse seems to have involved any active demonstration of support for the government comparable to that which Addison and, to a lesser extent, Steele would perform as a matter of course. There is no evidence, for example, to connect him with the Kit-Kat Club during his stay in England. Swift was concerned not with political activity of this sort but with using his influence with the government to obtain benefits for the Church and preferment for himself. His point of view on public issues was governed generally by such considerations and did not necessarily coincide with that of his Whig friends. Consequently, the following account of Swift's personal relations with Addison and Steele in the period 1707–09 will necessarily be a record also of his efforts in support of the Church and his increasing resentment of the ecclesiastical policies of the Whigs.

1.

Within a week of his arrival in England Swift wrote Archbishop King about the prospects for success in his efforts to gain a remission of the First Fruits. He requested permission to "engage the good offices" of any important officials with whom he had credit, especially Lord Somers and the Earl of Sunderland, "because the former by his great influence, and the other by his employment and alliance, may be very instrumental." King agreed, and it may be assumed that Swift at once broached the matter to these friends in high station. On January 1, however, he was writing again to King, in terms somewhat less sanguine, of an ominous development in the negotiations:

> I have heard it whispered by some who are fonder of political refinements than I, that a new difficulty may arise in this matter, that it must perhaps be purchased by a compliance with what was undertaken and endeavoured in Ireland last sessions, which I confess I cannot bring myself yet to believe, nor do I care to think or reason upon it.[2]

His reference is to the attempts made in Ireland to repeal the Sacramental Test clause, which prevented non-Anglicans from holding public office. The English government had for several years done little to aid the dissenters in their efforts to secure the repeal of this clause, although such efforts constituted the chief political activity of the Irish Presbyterians. In 1707, however, the possibility of an invasion focused the attention of the Whigs once more on the condition of Ireland. In his speeches before the opening session of the Irish Parliament in July, the Earl of Pembroke, then Lord Lieutenant, made a clear hint in favor of repeal, a hint which was overwhelmingly opposed by Parliament the following month.[3] Swift, in his letter to King, is voicing his first suspicion of what to him could be only an extremely unpleasant development: that the latest Whig maneuver for securing the repeal of the test was to make support for such a repeal the only condition by which the Irish clergy could obtain the grant of the First Fruits. For the moment he was merely dismayed; it remained for the truth of the rumor to stir him into active opposition to this proposal of his powerful Whig friends.

In January, 1707/8, Swift's hopes for his own preferment likewise suffered a setback. Somers had recommended him for the see of Waterford, and his nomination had received the support of the Archbishop of Canterbury. He was soon informed, however, that the appointment had fallen to Dr. Thomas Milles, whom he ironically characterized as "an ornament to the order, and a public blessing to the Church and nation." [4] This was merely the first of a number of similar disappointments which kept him in suspense during the last three years of the Whig hegemony. Sir Charles Firth, while unable to suggest a specific reason for the first disappointment, has shown that the general obstacle during this period was not Swift's authorship of the *Tale of a Tub,* as has sometimes been thought, but his failure to support the removal of the Irish test clause. "He was ill-used, as he truly said, for not being Whiggish enough." [5]

Thus, a month before the first meeting with Addison and Steele of which we have any record, Swift had encountered the two areas which were to be the principal sources of his later discontent with the Whigs. Nonetheless, he had as yet no real reason for resentment, and he moved with some enthusiasm into the world of wit and conversation which centered around Addison and Steele.

On February 29, 1707/8, Addison wrote Swift requesting his company for dinner the next day; the group would include Steele and Philip Frowde. As Ball points out, the language of this letter, the first between them which is extant, indicates that they had only recently become acquainted.[6] As they met, the political situation was undergoing some change. A complete Whig victory had resulted from the ministerial crisis precipitated by the efforts of the Queen and Harley to dismiss Godolphin and form a moderate Tory government. Marlborough promptly resigned, and a "middle party" of ministers refused to act without him. Harley, whose position had been weakened by the arrest of his secretary, William Greg, on charges of treason, was forced to resign on February 11. The subsequent changes in the ministry considerably strengthened the control of the Whig Junto over the policies of the government.[7]

It is interesting to compare the separate accounts which Swift and Addison give of these developments. Swift, writing to King the day after Harley's resignation, recounts the series of events fairly objectively, with little show of any personal involvement. If anything he seems somewhat aloof from the embroilment of party politics: "I never in my life saw or heard such divisions and complications of parties as there have been for some time: you sometimes see the extremes of Whig and Tory driving on the same thing." [8] Addison, as might be expected, sees the situation with the eyes of one much more thoroughly committed to the Whig point of view:

> It is said Mr Harley and his friends had laid schemes to undermine most of our Great officers of State and plant their own party in the room of 'em. . . . It is I believe very certain that the Duke of Marlborough and Lord Treasurer refused to sit any longer in Council with so wily a secretary and woud have laid down themselves if he had not been removed. . . . This Revolution has already had the good Effect to Unite all old friends that were falling off from one another, and in all probability will produce a good new Parlament.[9]

This difference in the attitude of Addison and Swift toward a political crisis at the time of their earliest acquaintance does not arise from any conflict of principle. It results merely from a difference in perspective, in point of view, between a clergyman concerned primarily with political matters as they affect the Church and an Undersecretary whose support of a specific political group was unhesitating. It is a nice distinction, perhaps, but a significant one.

Swift was, in fact, courted by Addison and Steele more as a wit and conversationalist than as a fellow Whig, although his connections with Somers, Halifax, and Sunderland would naturally have recommended him. Addison's most recent biographer, Peter Smithers, has a rather curious view of this early relationship. He writes that Swift "took pride in placing himself upon an equal footing of intimacy with the two other members of the 'trium-virate,' who enjoyed a political and literary reputation with which his own was as yet in no way comparable." [10] This is surely an overstatement. By this time, early in 1708, Addison and Steele would have known Swift as the author of *A Tale of a Tub* and of the *Contests and Dissensions.* And they certainly were well acquainted with his role as Isaac Bickerstaff, whose first pamphlet, *Predictions for the Year 1708,* had appeared in January.

There is no need to review here the various steps in the punishment of John Partridge by the wits, but one or two aspects of the affair may be mentioned which have relevance to Swift's friendship with Addison and Steele at the time of its inception. For one thing, it is worth emphasizing once more that his satiric attack on Partridge was not merely a *jeu d'esprit* for the amusement of his coffeehouse acquaintance. As Herbert Davis has pointed out, one motive of Swift's satire was to punish Partridge for his abuse of the English clergy. It was on just this basis that George Parker had called for an attack on the astrologer:

> I hope some able Polite Pen of the Church of England, will . . . Chastise this Calumniating Libertine, and not suffer him to pass without Reproof for these his horrid Scandals. . . .[11]

Viewed in this light, the Bickerstaff papers are wholly consonant with the major part of Swift's literary activities in 1708, which were exactly those of an "able Polite Pen of the Church of England." But it was the "inimitable spirit and humour" of these pieces which won the admiration of Steele and Addison and, as Steele says, raised the name of Bickerstaff to "as high a pitch of reputation as it could possibly arrive at." [12] Steele, it may be added, is sometimes said to have played a leading role along with Swift in the attack on Partridge. However, none of the contributions to the jest can be ascribed to him except his occasional sallies as Isaac Bickerstaff in the *Tatler* a year and a half later. There is no reason, in other words, to consider the Bickerstaff papers as a collaborative effort of Swift and the Whig wits with whom he was becoming intimate.

Swift's letters of the summer and early fall of 1708 give an incomplete but convincing picture of his increasing prominence in this group of friends, which included Rowe, Congreve, Anthony Henley, Philip Frowde, and Ambrose Philips. From many sporadic references we may observe his friendship with Addison and Steele becoming increasingly close. In July, for example, he wrote to Philips of "the triumvirate of Mr. Addison, Steele, and me," which is the remark that so arouses Mr. Smithers's ire. Again, in September, he praised Addison in another letter to Philips in these terms:

> That man has worth enough to give reputation to an age, and all the merit I can hope for with regard to you, will be my advice to cultivate his friendship to the utmost, and my assistance to do you all the good offices towards it in my power.[13]

It was probably also during this year that Swift received from Addison a copy of his *Remarks on Several Parts of Italy,* inscribed to "the most agreeable companion, the truest friend, and the greatest genius of his age." [14] From 1708, too, date Addison's revisions of Swift's poem *Baucis and Philemon.*

Swift seems never to have held Steele in quite as high regard as he did Addison, but they were certainly on close terms at this time. We find, for example, that Swift was very much at home in the Gazetteer's office and on one occasion, at least, exerted influence on the choice of material to be included in the *Gazette.* Referring to the battle of Lille, Swift wrote on August 28:

> In the last Gazette it was certainly affirmed that there would be a battle: but the copy coming to the office to be corrected I prevailed with them to let me soften the phrase a little, so as to leave some room for possibilities. . . .[15]

Steele was probably wise to take Swift's advice in this instance, since his accounts of the events at Lille were naturally read with great attention and some dissatisfaction. "A desponding paragraph about Lille was published in a late *Gazette,*" complained one correspondent at the time, and Anthony Henley had this report to make to Swift from his home in Hampshire:

> I do not know how Steele will get off of it: his veracity is at stake in Hampshire. Pray desire him to take the town, though he should leave the citadel for a nest-egg.

Steele was, in fact, publicly charged in Defoe's *Review* with mishandling the news from Lille.[16]

At the same time that Swift was thus consolidating his friendship with the Whig literary figures, he was pursuing the grant of the First Fruits with a growing sense of frustration. It was becoming increasingly clear to him that as the price of the First Fruits the Whig ministry demanded the consent of the Irish clergy to the repeal of the Test. On April 15 he wrote King that Somers had requested his opinion of the Test Act, which he had given him frankly but tactfully, since Somers was valued both as a friend and as a possible instrument for securing the First Fruits. To Dean Stearne on the same day Swift expressed his alarm at the activity of Alan Brodrick, the Whig speaker of the House of Commons in Ireland, who was then in England soliciting for the repeal of the Test clause by an act of the English Parliament. Swift angrily demanded Brodrick's impeachment and called for an address from the Irish clergy "to set the Queen and Court right about the Test." Moreover, he announced to King his intention of publishing a paper in opposition to the repeal of the Test, should that project be undertaken in the next session of the English Parliament.[17]

On the advice of Somers and with the assistance of Sunderland, Swift now sought an interview with the Lord Treasurer himself, Earl Godolphin. This talk with the highest official of the cabinet, which occurred in June, confirmed Swift's suspicions that the ministry intended to barter the First Fruits for a repeal of the Test. Godolphin assured him that the grant could be made if it were received with "due acknowledgments," a phrase which Swift was at no loss to interpret. His interview with Godolphin, as Professor Landa points out, "was a turning point in Swift's relations with the Whigs. It was a moment of decision, in which he had to choose whether he should retain the principles he believed beneficial to the Church of Ireland or whether he should make a sacrifice to political expediency."[18] To the possible detriment of his chances for preferment Swift refused to compromise his convictions in this matter. For the moment he felt his usefulness as a negotiator was over, and he left the affair to be managed by the Irish Lord Lieutenant, the Earl of Pembroke. In August he wrote King a report frankly skeptical of Pembroke's claims of progress but indicating that he still felt the best role for himself was one of tactful silence: "In the mean time, I have not stirred a step further; being unwilling to ruin myself in any man's favour, when I can do the public no good." [19]

2.

In a letter of September 14 to Ambrose Philips, Swift makes a remark which reveals another important phase of his activities in 1708. He rallies Philips about Shaftesbury's *Letter Concerning Enthusiasm:*

> There has been an essay of Enthusiasm lately published. . . . All my friends will have me to be the author, *sed ego non credulus illis.* By the free Whiggish thinking I should rather take it to be yours; but mine it is not, for though I am every day writing by speculations in my chamber, they are quite of another sort.[20]

These "by speculations" are usually taken to mean his writings on political and ecclesiastical subjects which date from this period. They are indeed "quite of another sort" from "free Whiggish thinking," since, taken together, they represent an essentially moderate point of view, one which on many issues runs directly counter to the measures then being pressed by the Whig government. In fact, Swift later adduced these works as evidence that he had never been a "favourer of the low-party":

> Whereas it hath been manifest to all men, that, during the highest dominion of that faction, I had published several tracts in opposition to the measures then taken: For instance, A Project for the Reformation of Manners . . . ; The Sentiments of a Church-of-England man; an Argument against abolishing Christianity; and, lastly, a Letter to a Member of Parliament against taking off the Test in Ireland. . . .[21]

Actually, the circumstances of composition and publication of these tracts are a bit more complicated than Swift indicates. Only the *Letter Concerning the Sacramental Test* and the *Project for the Advancement of Religion and the Reformation of Manners* were published during this period of Whig rule, the others appearing first in the *Miscellanies* of 1711.[22]

That his original intention in 1708 was to publish all these works at that time, along with his *Remarks* on Tindal's *Rights of the Christian Church* (never completed), is shown by a list he made in October or November of that year, headed "Subjects for a Volume." This list comprised most of the pieces which later appeared in the *Miscellanies,* including all these tracts on Church and State except the pamphlet on the Test, which was composed a month after the list was drawn up. And the fact remains that with one exception all these essays were composed in 1708 and to some extent serve to justify Swift's claims of political consistency. The single exception is *The Sentiments of a Church-of-England Man,* which may have been composed as early as 1704; [23] however, Swift clearly thought of it as relevant to events in 1708, since he included it in his list for a proposed volume and later dated it 1708.

The essays which were written but not published during this period of his closest alliance with the Whigs are quite significant and deserve brief mention here, even though they presumably could have had no impact at the time. They all reveal Swift's essentially moderate position on political and ecclesiastical affairs. In *The Sentiments of a Church-of-England Man,* long regarded as the fundamental expression of his principles, Swift places himself as Churchman above both political parties, finding much to deplore in the extremism which encourages dissenters to align themselves with the Whigs and the Papists or Non-Jurors with the Tories. The Whigs are castigated especially for their encouragement of intemperate attacks on the clergy. In matters of government, however, he is more sympathetic to the so-called "Whig" point of view. He defends the Revolution Settlement and the Protestant Succession against the arguments of the Non-Jurors. Swift's judicious conclusion is that to preserve the Constitution in Church and State, "whoever hath a true Value for both, would be sure to avoid the Extreams of *Whig* for the Sake of the former, and the Extreams of *Tory* on Account of the latter." [24]

The other two tracts composed but not printed at this time are also primarily defenses of the Church. The first, Swift's unfinished *Remarks* on Tindal's *Rights of the Christian Church,* attempts to reconcile the divine right of the Church with Whig political principles. His solution rests upon a distinction between the divine power of the clergy and the liberty of exercising that power, which is only by the permission of the civil government.[25] The second essay is his famous ironic *Argument* against the abolishing of Christianity in England. This piece need not be analyzed here, but it should be realized that one of its primary purposes is to warn the Whig leaders of the dangers which would result from the repeal of the Test clause. In fact, the "repeal of Christianity" is to be equated throughout with the repeal of the Test.[26]

Neither this open opposition to specific Whig proposals nor Swift's moderate position on ecclesiastical and political issues seems to have had any effect on his close friendship with Addison and Steele in 1708. Indeed, his conviction that a "Church-of-England man" should be essentially independent of any political party would have made it difficult for him to conceive of his own personal relationships being damaged by the "Spirit of Faction." In the *Sentiments* he makes his personal indifference to party allegiance quite plain:

> I converse in full Freedom with many considerable Men of both Parties; and if not in equal Number, it is purely accidental and personal, as happening to be near the Court, and to have made Acquaintance there, more under one Ministry than another.[27]

Of course allowance must be made both for the rhetorical purposes of such a statement and the early date of its composition; in 1708 it is doubtful that Swift felt himself to be quite this non-political, since he hoped to gain advantages for himself and his Church through his Whig connections. Even so, in these pamphlets of 1708 he emerges as a Churchman first of all, not a partisan, and in this he contrasts markedly with such friends as Steele, whose appointment as Gazetteer had been a political move by the Junto,[28] or Addison, now a Whig member for Lostwithiel as well as Undersecretary, or Anthony Henley, also a strong Whig representative in Commons. It is a measure of Swift's unwillingness to think of his friendships in political terms that he should have originally considered publishing his *Miscellanies*, including these tracts on Church and State, with a preface by Steele. When the work finally appeared in 1711, this idea was abandoned; by that time political differences could no longer be ignored.

3.

In the last two months of 1708 political events once again forced Swift to examine his relationship with the Whigs. The death of the Prince Consort on October 28 resulted in the final successful step in the Junto's efforts to gain control of all important cabinet posts. Prince George had been Lord High Admiral; upon his death that office was filled by Pembroke, whose two posts of Lord Lieutenant of Ireland and President of the Council were then open for Wharton and Somers respectively.

For Swift these developments were both promising and disconcerting. They meant, as he put it, "that most of those I have credit with will come into play," and that consequently his efforts to obtain preferment and his solicitations on behalf of the Church would be more favorably received. At the same time, however, his opposition to the ecclesiastical policies of the Whigs was unyielding, and he feared that the new power which the Junto had gained would encourage them to "carry things too far." [29] He wrote at once to Archbishop King, intimating that his friends among the Whigs might seek to put his literary talents to use, but assuring him that his principles as a Churchman would remain unchanged. He also expressed to King the hope that he would be removed from the political scene by an assignment to Vienna as Queen's Secretary in the company of the Earl of Berkeley. This opportunity, however, was never given him, although he must have been expecting the appointment for some months. Instead, he remained in London, in the midst of this "new world" of Whig power, a world in which his own position was somewhat paradoxical. At the end of November he was erroneously led to believe that the First Fruits had been granted, and he reported the news to King with an ironic reflection on the Church policy of the Whigs:

> I hope you are prepared to take off the Sacramental Test, because that will be a means to have it taken off here among us; and that

the clergy will be for it, in consideration of the Queen's bounty; and that men in employment will be so wise as to please the Court, and secure themselves. . . .[30]

Swift's suspicions were increased by the appointment of the Earl of Wharton as Lord Lieutenant of Ireland. Wharton was known to be the member of the Junto most favorable to the interests of the dissenters, and Swift, like everyone else, saw his appointment as the sign of further Whig efforts to repeal the Test in Ireland. The Irish Presbyterians found in Wharton's appointment a source of considerable pleasure; Archbishop King wrote of "the insolency and impudence of the dissenters on the encouragement they fancied to themselves in the change of the government here." [31] And the Whig *Observator* confidently predicted "strenuous Endeavours from his Lordship to put all the *Irish* Protestants in an equal Capacity to defend the Protestant and *British* Interest in that Kingdom." [32] The change in Lord Lieutenants could only have deepened Swift's distrust of the Whigs in matters affecting the Church.

For his friends Addison and Steele, however, Wharton's appointment had somewhat different results. Aside from the pleasure which they probably felt at the final success of the Junto's strategy, both had reason to expect material advantage from the ministerial changes. On December 6 Addison was appointed Chief Secretary to Wharton and was assured of a seat in the Irish Parliament. Steele immediately saw his chance, for on the same day he wrote to his wife that he hoped to succeed Addison as Undersecretary to Sunderland. Addison sought to gain Wharton's influence on behalf of his friend, but his efforts were unsuccessful. On December 28 Peter Wentworth reported to his brother that Sunderland had put off Steele "with a promise to get him the next place he shall ask that may be keep [sic] with his Gazette." [33]

It had been suggested to Swift by Archbishop King that he, too, should take advantage of Wharton's appointment by applying for the position of Chaplain to the Lord Lieutenant, although King was careful to express his conviction that Swift was "too honest to come on ill terms." He made no application for the post, however, and Wharton appointed as his chaplain the Reverend Ralph Lambert, whose recent sermon urging a

closer union of the Church with the dissenters made him eminently acceptable to the Whig Lord Lieutenant.[34]

Swift's irritation at this development was increased by the
hostile attitude toward the affairs of the Church of Ireland then
prevalent in the Whig newspapers. Agitation in those quarters
for repeal of the Test Act increased to the degree that Swift was
soon moved to state in print his unalterable opposition to this
favorite scheme of his Whig acquaintances. It was the *Observator*
which led the attack in the Whig press, and it did so in a manner
especially offensive to Swift. The prosecution that fall of two
Presbyterian ministers for preaching in Drogheda was taken by
that paper as "plain Proof" that "Popery and *Jacobitism* have
increas'd more of late in *Ireland*." [35] For three issues the *Observator* attempted to make a *cause célèbre* of this affair and directly attacked both Archbishop King and Primate Marsh. It was
easy enough to impugn the Test clause in such a context, and
the *Observator*, which had been demanding its repeal all year,
now closed its discussion of the Drogheda prosecutions by calling
for the deliverance of Irish Presbyterians from "those Oppres-
sions, and from that Note of Bastardy lately impos'd upon them
by the Sacramental Test." [36] Swift saw in such a statement further
confirmation of his suspicion that the Junto would soon intensify its efforts to repeal the Test, a suspicion which on November 30 he communicated to Archbishop King by writing
ironically in the guise of a Whig:

> The Archbishop of Dublin is represented here as one that will very
> much oppose our designs; and, although I will not say that the
> "Observator" is paid for writing as he does; yet I can positively
> affirm to you, that whatever he says of that Archbishop, or of the
> affairs of Ireland, or those here, is exactly agreeable to our thoughts
> and intentions.[37]

Less than a week later Swift publicly entered the controversy
with *A Letter from a Member of the House of Commons in Ireland to a Member of the House of Commons in England, Concerning the Sacramental Test*, dated December 4.[38] Biographically, this tract is of considerable importance. It is the first
published work of this period in which Swift takes a completely
independent position in political matters, and it is a position

considerably at odds with that of the Whig government. He insists, for example, that the question of the Test is properly a concern of the Irish government, not the English. His basic assumption, here and in his other writing on the subject, is that the dissenters must be prevented from gaining any political power by which the national Church could be subverted. Characteristically, his method in support of this position is to carry matters to their logical extreme by depicting a state of affairs in which the dissenters have gained control of Parliament, made themselves the national Church, and refused toleration to the "dissenting Episcopals." Moreover, Swift does not hesitate to admonish the Whig ministers for their role in the affair. He makes it clear that they are responsible for the tactics of the *Observator,* including the objectionable attack on Archbishop King. And he takes considerable pains to show that his argument in favor of the Test clause is entirely consistent with the principles of an "old" Whig, who accepts the Revolution, the Protestant Succession, and the doctrines and discipline of the Church of England. For the purposes of this tract he has assumed the character of a Whig member of Parliament, and in his demonstration that efforts to repeal the Test in Ireland are destined to fail, he is careful to show that all those who will oppose it, including most of his fellow members in Commons, the Bishops in Lords, and the body of the clergy, are "good *Whigs,* in our Acceptation of the Word." Swift seeks in this way to warn the Whigs that a move to repeal the Test will be an unpopular one among those of their own party in Ireland.

There can be no doubt that the appearance of the *Letter* had some impact on his relations with the Whig leaders; in a personal reference appearing only in the first edition, he writes of himself, "It may not be altogether improbable that his great Friends have dropp'd him, which Disappointment . . . may chance to cool his Zeal that way, if he had any before, of which I cannot accuse him." [39] Archbishop King had no difficulty in detecting Swift's hand in the tract, and neither, apparently, did the ministers. Swift later recounted that his authorship was suspected by Lambert, Wharton's chaplain, who communicated his suspicion to the Lord Lieutenant. Finally, the advertisement to the reprint of the tract in the *Miscellanies* of 1711 tells us that "the Suspicion which the supposed Author lay under for Writing this Letter, absolutely ruined him with the late M[ini]stry." [40]

It did not, however, "ruin" him with his friends. Early in January, Swift wrote King to recommend Addison as a "most excellent person" and his "most intimate friend." Since Addison would soon be leaving for Ireland, Swift attempted to give him a persuasive account of the all-important question of the Sacramental Test, and received from the new Secretary the assurance that Wharton would not attempt its repeal if that action should appear really unpopular. Although Addison was now "really a very great man with the juncto," as Peter Wentworth put it,[41] Swift seems to have become increasingly intimate with him during the first months of 1709. Letters from Swift to Robert Hunter, a prisoner in Paris, show him constantly in Addison's company in these weeks, especially at St. James coffeehouse. In his efforts to conclude his affairs as Sunderland's Undersecretary and make the necessary preparations for departure to Ireland, Addison was then unusually involved in government business, which, however, he refused to discuss with Swift on the grounds that he was too close a friend.

In February Addison was able to use his official position to acquire information for Swift about the progress of the grant of First Fruits, although apparently he was reluctant to become too closely involved in the affair. Swift had first begun to suspect the accuracy of the earlier report that Pembroke had obtained the grant when Addison informed him that he had received no orders about it. Since Addison, who had also received a letter from Archbishop King on this business, seemed unwilling to press the matter, Swift himself inquired at the Treasury and discovered that such a grant had never been ordered. At the same time he made application to Wharton, Addison's superior and Pembroke's successor. Wharton, however, received him very coldly, possibly because he resented Swift's opposition to the repeal of the Test clause; this incident left Swift with a violent antipathy for Wharton, although for the moment he remained closer to the Earl than he later cared to admit. As for the First Fruits, Swift wrote King, "I observe such a reluctance in some friends whose credit I would employ, that I begin to think no farther of it." [42]

In the meantime, his literary activity had continued. The finishing touches had been put to the Bickerstaff hoax with *The Vindication of Isaac Bickerstaff, Esq.* and *A Famous Prediction of Merlin;* in April appeared *A Project for the Advancement of Religion and the Reformation of Manners.* This essay was immediately heralded by Steele in the fifth issue of his new periodical, the *Tatler.* "The author," writes Steele, "must certainly be a man of wisdom, as well as piety, and have spent much time in the exercise of both." [43] Now, Steele's praise was not merely a friendly gesture; there is much in the *Project* to gain his enthusiastic support. Swift, for example, demands that piety and virtue be made the necessary qualifications for preferment and temporal reward, and calls for reform in such specific areas as the theater, the universities, and even the alehouses. Very obviously, what he says here has much in common with the moral intentions of the *Tatler* itself. Yet there are surely some aspects of Swift's essay with which Steele would not have been sympathetic. For one thing, although the specific proposals are of the sort to win Steele's approval, Swift's underlying assumption here is that all men are dominated by self-love:

> For, if Religion were once understood to be the necessary Step to Favour and Preferment; can it be imagined, that any Man would openly offend against it, who had the least Regard for his Reputation or his Fortune? There is no Quality so contrary to any Nature, which Men cannot affect, and put on upon Occasion, in order to serve an Interest, or gratify a prevailing Passion: The proudest Man will personate Humility, the morosest learn to flatter, . . . where he is in pursuit of what he hath much at Heart: How ready therefore would most Men be to step into the Paths of Virtue and Piety, if they infallibly led to Favour and Fortune? [44]

As we have seen, this is not a view of human nature which Steele was inclined to share. Some commentators, whose suspicions are aroused by the term "project," have raised the question of the extent to which Swift is ironic in this essay, and W. B. Ewald, in particular, makes a valiant effort to characterize the *persona* of the tract. Undeniably there do occur occasional shifts of tone from serious to ironic, for the purpose of individual satiric thrusts.[45] Surely, however, it is sufficient to say that Swift's proposals are quite serious but that they arise from one central irony: the "depravities" which he describes are so "universal and deep-rooted" that the only feasible remedy must be based realistically on man's innate selfishness.

Moreover, the political implications of the *Project* are decidedly anti-Whig. Although Swift's early biographer Sheridan perhaps exaggerates when he describes the tract as "a very strong, though covert, attack, upon the power of the Whigs," [46] there is no doubt that Swift's intention here was largely political; the *Project* occupies the first place in his list in the *Memoirs* of works written against the Whigs while they were still in power. As Davis points out, in demanding "piety" as the criterion of promotion in government, Swift is supporting the authority of the Established Church and, by extension, arguing once more against the abolishing of the Sacramental Test.[47] The *Project* accumulates such political overtones as it goes along, and they gradually become more explicit. Swift asserts that a law limiting the press has been made necessary by the proliferation of "freethinking" books, "although," he writes, "it is to be supposed, that neither Party avow such Principles, or own the supporting of them to be any way necessary to their Service." [48] This is obviously ironic; he had already attacked the toleration by the Whigs of "Despisers of Religion and Revelation" in his *Sentiments of a Church-of-England Man*. Finally, at the end of the *Project,* he openly attacks the Church policy of the Junto:

> But, it must be confessed, That as Things are now, every Man thinks he hath laid in a sufficient Stock of Merit, and may pretend to any Employment, provided he hath been loud and frequent in declaring himself hearty for the Government. It is true he is a *Man of Pleasure,* and a *Free-Thinker;* that is, in other Words, he is profligate in his Morals, and a despiser of Religion; but in Point of Party, he is one to be *confided* in; he is an Asserter of Liberty and Property; he rattles it out against *Popery,* and *Arbitrary Power,* and *Priest Craft,* and *High-Church.* It is enough: He is a Person fully qualified for any Employment in the Court, or the Navy, the Law, or the Revenue. . . .[49]

Swift may have written the *Project* with the hope that it would aid him in obtaining preferment,[50] and the moral flavor of the piece won Steele's admiration; but its political implications are wholly consistent with his opposition in the period to the policies of the Whig ministry.

The *Project* was published in April; in that same month Steele began publication of the *Tatler*. Swift supplied him with the pseudonym Isaac Bickerstaff and also, apparently, with many hints and suggestions, although his actual contributions to the early numbers were probably limited to the single poem, "A Description of the Morning." He was, at any rate, popularly considered to have a major share in the authorship of the periodical. It is interesting to note that even at this time of Swift's greatest influence on the *Tatler*, Steele was using the work as an outlet for his political predilections. In the fourth issue he constructed a political allegory in praise of each member of the Whig Junto. He writes, for example, of "Verono," or Wharton, as follows:

> This minister is master of great abilities, and is as industrious and restless for the preservation of the liberties of the people, as the greatest enemy can be to subvert them.[51]

As we shall see, Steele was to use the *Tatler* for such political propaganda to an increasing extent in the next two years. He was, in fact, satirized at some time during this year in a broadside which accuses the "top Whiggs" of choosing *"Britain's Censor for their Tool."* [52]

While Steele was proclaiming his support of the ministry in the *Tatler*, Addison was beginning his service as Secretary to Wharton in Ireland. He had arrived in Dublin on April 21 and had written a friendly letter to Swift almost at once, expressing the hope that he would soon see Swift in Ireland. In the meantime, he was busily engaged in preparations for the opening of the Irish Parliament. Wharton's opening speech to Parliament on May 5 was watched with a good deal of attention, since it was thought that he would then demand the repeal of the Test clause. Such, however, was not the case. The Lord Lieutenant was too circumspect and diplomatic to provoke the formidable opposition which awaited such a move. Addison's account to Halifax of that speech is revelatory both of his thorough support of Wharton and of his attitude toward the issue which so engrossed Swift:

> Your Lordship will see by them that all parties here set out in good humour which is entirely owing to His Ex^cy's conduct who has addressed himself to all sorts of men since his arrival here with unspeakable application. They were under great apprehensions at his first coming that He woud drive directly at repealing the Test and had formed themselves into a very strong Body for its defence, but as their minds are at present pretty quiet upon that Head they appear willing to Enter into all other measures that he woud have them.

He then intimates that the repeal of the Test may still be achieved:

> His Ex^cy however gains ground daily and I question not but in a new parlament where parties are not settled and confirmed He will be able to Lead them into anything that will be for their Real Interest and Advantage.[53]

The *Observator,* it may be noted, had the same interpretation to make of Wharton's speech and took advantage of the occasion to demand once more that the Test in Ireland be repealed.

Swift had resolved to return to Ireland in June, but before leaving England he made another gesture toward securing Whig support for his preferment. In a flattering letter he asked Halifax to keep Somers reminded of him and to use his influence to obtain him a place in England. He then made preparations for departure; Addison wrote to him at Chester offering the service of a government yacht for the crossing, but the letter arrived too late. Swift sailed at his own expense, arriving in Ireland on June 30.

At the end of this visit of almost two years in England Swift was still a nominal Whig, at least as far as his personal associations were concerned. He still looked for preferment from his "great friends," and he was now on intimate terms with Addison and Steele, as well as with the other "Whig wits." But on another, and less superficial, level the events of this period had left him fairly disillusioned about the policies of the Godolphin ministry and the value of his Whig connections. While Addison and Steele were consolidating their position as rising Whig politicians, Swift was expending his efforts in support of his Church. In such a role his distrust of the Whigs increased, and the controversy over the Sacramental Test brought him into active opposition to the Junto. Swift's alignment a year later with the Harley ministry and the subsequent break with Addison and Steele are firmly grounded in his refusal in these years to sacrifice his convictions for the sake of political expediency.

2

SWIFT'S CHANGE OF
PARTIES, 1709-1710

I N HIS OWN DAY a charge of political apostasy was commonly made
against Swift by his enemies, and it still appears occasionally. In 1715, after the accession of George I had returned the
Whigs to political power, John Oldmixon made the accusation
in its typical form:

> *Swift* had been very conversant with the *Whigs,* had written several
> *Tatlers,* and some *Whig* Lampoons, had offer'd his Service to the
> Earl of *Godolphin,* to write for him, before he prostituted his Pen
> to his Lordship's Successor.[1]

Political partisans seldom have the inclination to analyze the
rationale of their opponents, and for the Whigs who felt the
power of Swift's pen his alignment with the Tories in 1710 remained a sudden, unprincipled, mercenary act.

That Addison and Steele to some degree shared the general
Whig estimate of their former friend was a source of genuine
regret to Swift, who made sincere efforts to keep politics from
infecting his personal relationships. His efforts to obtain advantages for Addison and Steele from his friends among the new

ministry were viewed as sheer arrogance by the Whig wits, although they were not unwilling to accept whatever aid he could
procure. It was soon evident to Swift that "the curse of party"
had made inevitable the collapse of his friendship with the two
leading Whig literary figures.

Swift and Addison, however, were able to spend a friendly
year together in Ireland before the ministerial crisis which precipitated their personal crisis. This chapter will consider that
more pleasant association before tracing Swift's relationship
with his two friends in the period when his distrust of the
Junto increased to the point of alliance with their political
opponents.

1.

Although the records of Swift's life in Ireland during the summer of 1709 are very few, it is clear that he was in Addison's
company whenever the Secretary's busy schedule would allow.
In July, for example, Addison was able to visit Swift on his
return from Wharton's country home at Chapelizod, but such
occasions were more rare than either could wish. Addison was
thoroughly immersed in the affairs of Wharton's government,
which was steadily winning more influence in the Irish Parliament, and in some ways his political activity could hardly
have been completely to Swift's taste. Years later Swift wrote
of Addison's dissatisfaction with the Irish Whigs:

> I remember my excellent friend Mr. Addison, when he first came
> over hither Secretary to the Earl of Wharton then Lord Lieutenant,
> was extremely offended at the conduct and discourse of the Chief
> Managers here: He told me they were a sort of people who seemed
> to think, that the principles of a Whig consisted in nothing else but
> damning the Church, reviling the Clergy, abetting the Dissenters,
> and speaking contemptibly of revealed Religion.[2]

In reality, however, Addison's complaint was not that the Whigs
in Ireland were too extreme but that they were too conservative. Thus he writes to Sunderland of the party which gave the
strongest support to Wharton:

> They all call themselves Whiggs but I don't believe that halfe of
> them woud goe such lengths as their friends in England coud wish

if there were any Occasion to trye them but My Ld Lieu^ts: Influence spreads among them dayly and I Question not but in a New Parliament he wou'd be able to worke them to any thing that wou'd be for theire security and hapiness.[3]

Moreover, Addison's letters of this period reveal his consistent support and apparent admiration for the Earl of Wharton, whom Swift later professed to hate "like a toad." To Godolphin, Somers, and Sunderland he carefully reported each step in the progress of Wharton's administration, ranging from the successful passage of the Money Bill to Wharton's efforts to prevent the lower house of Convocation from censuring a book by his Chaplain, Ralph Lambert.[4] At the end of the session on August 30, Commons voted an address of thanks to Wharton for his "good Administration," and in a few weeks he and Addison returned to England.

Once back in London Addison turned his attention to the question of Swift's preferment. On October 5, he dined with Steele, Maynwaring, Lord Halifax, Lord Essex, and Lord Russel, and, as Steele reported a few days later to Swift, "no man could say more in praise of another, than he did in your behalf" on this occasion. Halifax immediately sent Swift a letter containing glowing promises. Swift wrote a flattering reply early in November, but despite these polite, informal negotiations there were no signs of any advancement for Swift; his letter from Halifax was later sardonically endorsed, "I kept this letter as a true original of courtiers and Court promises."[5] He remained in Ireland, while Addison and Steele in London enjoyed the conversation of the coffeehouses and occupied themselves with the publication of the *Tatler*.

By this time Steele had openly shown his Whig colors in that periodical. In the early numbers he had been cautious and tactful in the introduction of political material, but in midsummer of 1709 the *Tatler* came to the aid of a Whig champion, Benjamin Hoadly, in his dispute with a High Church Tory, Bishop Blackall. Blackall's sermon before the Queen in March, which was answered by Hoadly, had been a strong statement of the doctrines of nonresistance and passive obedience to the magistrate, who has divine authority. In August Steele's *Tatlers* No. 44 and No. 50 supported Hoadly by satirizing Blackall as

Martin Powell, a puppeteer at Bath; a manipulator of puppets had obvious advantages as an allegorical figure for an advocate of nonresistance to authority.[6]

If Swift was aware of this controversy, he made no mention of it. As far as the issues themselves were concerned, he would not have been particularly sympathetic to Blackall's doctrines; he had made his own moderate position quite plain in *The Sentiments of a Church-of-England Man,* where he asserts that passive obedience is due to the Legislature, not to the Prince. Yet there were personalities involved as well as principles, and Hoadly, even before he attacked the Establishment in the Bangorian controversy, was a symbol for Whig extremism. As such, it may be noted, Swift later took pains to castigate him in the context of his most bitter attack on Steele, *The Public Spirit of the Whigs.* By December of 1709, Hoadly had gained enough prominence from his opposition to Blackall to be praised in the Whig House of Commons which on the same day was passing a resolution against Dr. Henry Sacheverell. It was another of Swift's friends, Anthony Henley, who on December 14 moved the address to Queen Anne urging her to bestow some Church dignity on Hoadly "for his eminent Services both to Church and State." [7]

Shortly thereafter the Whig ministers embarked on a course which was to prove fatal, the trial of Sacheverell. The provocation for the impeachment was his sermon of November 5, which reflected upon Godolphin as a wily "Volpone" and seemingly attacked the Revolution Settlement by its assertion of the principles of passive obedience and nonresistance. His trial in February and March became a political event of the first importance, and the cry of "Church in danger" resulted in riots and agitation. The effect of the trial was a great loss of popular support for the Whigs; their early defeat seemed almost certain.[8]

While the Sacheverell trial was in progress, Steele's *Tatler* maintained a discreet silence. There were no political papers at all in these months. Addison's contributions became more frequent, and either he or some official of the ministry may have been partly responsible for Steele's circumspection. However, shortly before the proceedings against Sacheverell were initiated, Steele had once again made a public demonstration of his political affiliations. He had been appointed a Commissioner of the Stamp Office in January, and, perhaps in gratitude, he devoted *Tatler* No. 130 (February 4, 1709/10) to a eulogy of the entire Whig administration. Typical of the indirection by which he achieves this result is the following comment, which is obviously meant to refer to Wharton:

> Were we to form to ourselves the idea of one whom we would think proper to govern a distant kingdom, consisting chiefly of those who differ from us in religion, and are influenced by foreign politics, would it not be such a one as had signalised himself by a uniform and unshaken zeal for the Protestant interest, and by his dexterity in defeating the skill and artifice of its enemies? [9]

Similar praise was extended to Orford, Cowper, Somers, and Godolphin; later this year, the Tories were to remember Steele's excursion into politics in this particular issue of the *Tatler*.

At about the same time, Addison's political career was proceeding successfully, after a temporary setback in December, 1709, when his election as a member from Lostwithiel was declared invalid in the House, on the grounds that the borough franchise had been incorrectly interpreted. However, on March 11, 1709/10, he was elected a member from Malmesbury. This borough was dominated by Wharton, and apparently it was largely through his influence that Addison's election there was secured.[10]

While his friends were becoming committed more deeply than ever to the support of the Junto, Swift remained somewhat aloof from the world of party politics. The only political piece to come from his pen at this time was *A Letter to a Member of Parliament in Ireland Upon Chusing a new Speaker there*, which was written, but apparently not published, early in 1710. Once again, this tract illustrates Swift's unalterable opposition to the direction which the policies of the Junto took in matters affecting the Church. "You know very well," he writes, "the great Business of the High-flying Whigs, at this Juncture, is to endeavor a Repeal of the Test Clause." Since the majority of the members of the House are moderate men who favor the Test, he points out, it would be absurd to choose a Speaker who is against it, much less one who "should prove to be a Sollicitor, an Encourager, or even a Penner of Addresses to complain of it." [11] By those epithets Swift probably seeks to recall the activities of Alan Brodrick, the former Speaker who in 1708 had actively solicited the repeal of the Test. Such a mistake, he implies, must not be made again, and therefore the choice of a Speaker is necessarily a party issue, however distasteful the drawing of party lines may be. The new Speaker must be one whose position on the Test is in accord with that of the majority in Commons; to make a choice on any other grounds, such as to select merely the best parliamentarian available, would have disastrous effects outside the House as well as within. For one thing, the dissenters, who went to extreme lengths when hearing of a "new Friend in Office" (i.e., Wharton), would again be encouraged to flood the nation with pamphlets and sermons demanding the repeal of the Test or to go to more dangerous lengths. Finally, Swift launches into a discussion of the Test clause itself, which he defends on much the same basis as he had in his previous tract on the subject a year earlier.

It may be noted that the actual result of the election of a new Speaker was hardly gratifying to Swift. There was, as a matter of fact, no contest on the matter at all:

An honourable Member proposed the Honourable *John Forster,* her Majesty's Attorney General, as a fit person; and the Question being put by the Clerk, by Order of the Members, he was by general Consent chosen Speaker, and thereupon placed in the Chair.[12]

Forster (or Foster) was a zealous Whig; his speech in 1711 as the Recorder of Dublin to the Duke of Ormond on his arrival as Lord Lieutenant was parodied in a poem sometimes attributed to Swift. The "factual" section of Swift's *Short Character* of Wharton describes Forster as hand-picked by the Lord Lieutenant to be the Solicitor-General.[13] As it happened, the question of the Test did not arise in the House while Forster was Speaker. It seems unlikely, however, that his position on the matter would have satisfied Swift's demands in his unprinted pamphlet.

2.

On May 7, 1710, Addison and Wharton returned to Dublin to prepare for the opening of the Irish Parliament. In the following months Swift and Addison were able to see each other fairly often, especially in the company of their friends, St. George Ashe, Bishop of Clogher, and his brother Dillon Ashe, vicar of Finglas. In June, for example, Addison asked Swift, then at Laracor, to set out at once for Dublin, where they could enjoy the company of Dillon Ashe. He concluded, "I love your company and value your conversation more than any man's." [14] Apparently Addison this summer also made the acquaintance of Stella, who admired and perhaps imitated his practice of being "never positive in arguing." Had he not so soon afterwards left Ireland, he later assured Swift, "he would have used all endeavours to cultivate her friendship." [15]

While this friendly association was in progress, the entire political situation was undergoing a change. In April the Queen had replaced the Whig Lord Chamberlain, the Marquis of Kent, with the moderate Shrewsbury, who had voted against the ministry at Sacheverell's trial. At the beginning of the summer Harley's intrigue achieved another victory; on June 14, Sunderland, a leading member of the Junto and Addison's former superior, was dismissed and succeeded by the Tory Lord Dartmouth. It was clear to everyone that the fall of the Whigs had begun.[16]

Steele's reaction to these developments was to intensify his political campaign in the pages of the *Tatler,* primarily by extending indirect praise to the defeated Whigs and by satirizing the Tory leaders, especially Robert Harley. The issue of June 20 (No. 187) made oblique references to the mistreatment of Marlborough and the popular reaction to the Sacheverell trial, and two weeks later he defended his imprudence by depicting self-interest as contemptible "when the true public spirit of a nation is run into a faction against their friends and benefactors." [17] On June 29, he drew at length the character of a cunning man, "Polypragmon," which was generally taken as a satiric sketch of Harley, although Steele later denied any such intention. But the *Tatler* which excited the most attention as political satire was No. 193, which appeared on July 4. Here, in the guise of a letter from "Old Downes, the prompter," he attacks Harley's successful efforts to form a new ministry. Downes complains, for instance, that a "deep intriguer" has worked himself into the management of the theater and that "his restless ambition, and subtle machinations, did manifestly tend to the extirpation of the good old British actors, and the introduction of foreign pretenders; such as harlequins, French dancers, and Roman singers." This, of course, very thinly disguised, is simply the familiar Whig motif associating the Tories with the causes of Popery and Jacobitism. Steele's allegory continues with ridicule of the new ministers as "persons that never trod the stage before, and so very awkward and ungainly, that it is impossible to believe the audience will bear them." [18]

Steele later disclaimed the authorship of this paper, though not its political intention, which, obviously, was undeniable. A few days later he printed a letter, at one time incorrectly ascribed to Swift, which complained of his entrance into politics when so much work remained to be done in the reformation of manners. The writer, signing himself "Cato Junior," indicates where his political sympathies lie when he remarks that Bickerstaff has been led by passion into offending "the very better half of the nation." Steele defends himself on the ground that he is putting public spirit over self-interest; and it is certainly true that the "Letter from Downes" in the *Tatler* injured Steele's chances of retaining his offices under a new administration. Swift, in fact, believed that Steele's loss of the Gazetteership a few months later was a direct result of his publication of this essay.[19] It is an indication, also, of the damaging effect of *Tatler* No. 193 on Steele's career that a violent attack on Swift several years later accused him of having urged his friend to publish the letter from Downes, "which was the Beginning of his Ruin." [20] But Steele cared little for such consequences; he was committed, publicly and privately, to the support not only of Whig principles but also of individual Whig politicians, and he could not watch silently the disintegration of the Godolphin ministry.

This increasing willingness of Steele's to incorporate political materials into the *Tatler* did not go unnoticed by the opposition. On August 3 appeared the first number of the *Examiner,* which in the following months provided support for the new ministry of "moderates" being formed by Harley. In its early stages papers were supplied by a variety of hands, including St. John, Atterbury, and Prior. As early as the fifth number (August 31) Steele is censured, in an article entitled "The *Gazette* and *Tatler* of August the 12th Compared." The subject of that *Tatler* had been the victory of Stanhope, a Whig, in Spain, and the *Examiner* now warns Steele to restrict himself to observations on morality:

> No Body desires more than I do, that you should go on to expose Vice and Folly, and recommend Morality and Virtue, as agreeably as you can, and as often as you please. My Advice to you is only this, That you would still appear in your proper Sphere; . . . you mistake your Talent, whenever you meddle with Matters of State.[21]

In August, also, St. John's *Letter to the Examiner,* which trumpets the aims of the new ministry and urges the *Examiner* to expose the conduct of the Junto, cites Steele as an example of the "Weekly Poison" for which the *Examiner* is to furnish an antidote. The *Letter to the Examiner,* which also attacks the Kit-Kat Club, was soon answered by Lord Cowper, who uses St. John's attack on Steele as the excuse for his rebuttal. His tract is entitled *A Letter to Isaac Bickerstaff, Esq., Occasioned by the Letter to the Examiner.* Before replying to the arguments of St. John, Cowper praises Steele for his use of the *Tatler* "to expose some of those brutish notions of government, and vile arts of wretched pretenders to politics, which are the certain bane of national felicity." [22] Even before the change in government had really been completed, Steele was thus marked publicly as a loyal Whig, willing and able to serve his party in print.

In Ireland Addison was anxiously following the political crisis during the summer and awaiting an opportunity to return to London. He was concerned especially about the possibility of a dissolution of Parliament, which the Queen had announced would shortly occur. On August 5 he sounded a hopeful note: "We hear from all parts of England, that the people daily recover their senses, and that the tide begins to turn so strongly, that it is hoped the next parliament will be of the same stamp with this in case of a dissolution." [23] Such optimism was ill-founded; three days later the dismissal of Godolphin gave the deathblow to the government of the Junto, and there was every reason to expect popular approval of a new government in the event of a general election. By August 16 Addison had returned to England.

Swift, too, had taken stock of the rapidly changing political situation. As early as June 29 he had given a hint that he was well aware of the possibility of a future alignment with the Whigs' political opponents. In a letter of that date to Benjamin Tooke, a letter concerned primarily with the publication of the fifth edition of *A Tale of a Tub,* he made this significant remark:

> I have thoughts of some other work one of these years: and I hope to see you ere it be long; since it is likely to be a new world, and since I have the merit of suffering by not complying with the old.[24]

As yet, however, he was content merely to survey the situation; there was at that moment little opportunity for him even to consider any overt move toward finding a place for himself in this "new world."

In this letter to Tooke Swift also makes reference to the projected volume of his writings to contain, among other material, his tracts on Church and State composed in 1708. He had originally thought of publishing these with a preface by Steele, and Steele had reminded him of this fact in October of 1709: "I have not seen Ben Tooke a great while, but long to usher you and yours into the world." Now, however, in the early summer of 1710, Swift had certain misgivings about this phase of his plan for the *Miscellanies.* He wrote to Tooke, "I would not have you think of Steele for a publisher: he is too busy. I will, one of these days, send you some hints, which I would have in a preface, and you may get some friend to dress them up." [25] It is certainly unlikely that Swift's explanation for his change in plan is to be taken at face value. Although there was no real coolness between the two men this summer, the probability is that Swift was well aware of Steele's unequivocal support of the Junto in the political essays of the *Tatler.* His decision to look elsewhere for a preface perhaps arose less from any change in personal feeling toward Steele than from a growing realization of the inappropriateness of publishing such tracts as *A*

Letter Concerning the Sacramental Test or *The Sentiments of a Church-of-England Man* with an introduction by a determined Whig propagandist.

As a matter of fact, Steele paid Swift an extended compliment during this same summer. On July 10 the first volume of the collected *Tatler* appeared, and the dedication to that volume expresses the indebtedness of the *Tatler*'s "Isaac Bickerstaff" to the Isaac Bickerstaff whose predictions had made the name famous. In a letter to Addison Swift soon acknowledged the compliment as "very handsome." It should be noted, however, that the dedication containing the praise of Swift is addressed to Arthur Maynwaring, the Whig politician who was partly responsible for the intrusion of politics into the *Tatler* this summer and who soon was to secure Addison as the writer of the *Whig-Examiner*.

Swift, naturally enough, was anxious about the effect which the fall of the Whigs might have on his efforts to gain preferment. He received on July 23 letters from Steele and Halifax; they have not survived, but presumably they dealt with his expectations of advancement, since Addison urged their importance and Swift later acknowledged the "favour" Halifax proposed. A month later, on August 22, he wrote Addison to seek his advice about what future steps he should take to obtain preferment, in light of the present situation. In this letter he sympathizes with the "ill news" which Addison met on his return home, and reports, "Even the moderate Tories here are in pain at these revolutions, being what will certainly affect the Duke of Marlborough, and, consequently, the success of the war." [26] This is a fairly curious remark, coming as it does only a few months before Swift was to aid the new ministry in its attack upon Marlborough. Perhaps it is only a polite gesture for Addison's benefit; but perhaps too it is an index of Swift's uncertainty about his own position at this critical time. Like his apparently friendly relations with Wharton during the summer, such a remark may represent an attitude which he would soon be anxious to forget. At any rate, he goes on to ask Addison whether it is advisable for him to return to England. Wharton, he indicates, has told him that such a visit would accomplish nothing, since his friends there are no longer in a position to help him, but Swift finds some encouragement in the fact that Somers is still in office.

The problem of whether to return to England was resolved for him at the end of August. The Irish Bishops on August 31 decided to seek the remission of the First Fruits from the new ministry, and on that day Swift was again commissioned as their representative. Wharton was also preparing to leave Ireland, having told Swift that he did not expect to continue in office when his friends were out of power, and Swift departed in his company, arriving in England on September 1.

3.

On August 22 a *Tatler* by Steele, or possibly Addison, sarcastically proposed a State Weather-glass or barometer for the use of "supple" members of parties who change their pinciples according to the condition of the political atmosphere:

> When a man foresees a decaying ministry, he has leisure to grow a malcontent, reflect upon the present conduct, and by gradual murmurs fall off from his friends into a new party, by just steps and measures.[27]

Although Steele, at this early date, could not have been thinking of Swift in such a context, there is a certain irony in the applicability of this remark to his conduct only a month later. Addison and Steele, at any rate, were ready enough to believe that he had consulted a political barometer. For in September and October of 1710 Swift gradually became more closely associated with the leading figures of the new ministry, until in the beginning of November he took the final step of putting his literary talents at their service.

When he arrived in London on September 8, he found his position somewhat ambiguous. His business, again, was to solicit the remission of the First Fruits. But the "great friends" to whom he would ordinarily have applied were no longer "great," and he had as yet no real access to those who had succeeded them. Writing to Archbishop King the day after his arrival, he describes his difficulties as a political neutral:

> Upon my arrival here, I found myself equally caressed by both parties, by one as a sort of bough for drowning men to lay hold of;

and by the other as one discontented with the late men in power, for not being thorough in their designs, and therefore ready to approve present things.[28]

A visit to Godolphin, he goes on to report, resulted in "a reception very unexpected, . . . altogether short, dry, and morose." This personal rebuff certainly contributed to Swift's willingness to approve "present things," and on September 10 he reported to Stella that he had "talked treason heartily against the Whigs" and written some "hints," probably for *The Virtues of Sid Hamet the Magician's Rod,* his poem lampooning Godolphin. He continued, nonetheless, to visit his friends in the fallen ministry, Somers and Halifax. Somers had twice written to Wharton about him, Swift learned, only to have his solicitations ignored by the Lord Lieutenant.[29]

During the next month, however, the way was gradually opened for him to seek the grant of the First Fruits from the new men in power. As he had for the past two years, he felt that his own position in the current political warfare was that of an independent Churchman, seeking benefits for his Church and tied to no political party. Yet he was quick to recognize that the new government had in mind for him a role somewhat more significant than that of an "indifferent spectator," as he had described himself to Stella. In early October he met with Harley, and from this point on there was no question that he had abandoned any pretence of impartiality. Thus, on October 13, he speaks of his "cast Whigs" and makes this resolution: "I have done with them, and they have, I hope, done with this kingdom for our time." [30] Finally, on October 21, Harley informed him that the long-sought First Fruits had been granted by the Queen. The mission which had brought Swift to England was now accomplished, but he was no longer particularly eager to return to Ireland. When Harley explained that the great difficulty of the Tories "lay in the want of some good pen, to keep up the spirit raised in the people, to assert the principles, and justify the proceedings of the new ministers," [31] Swift promised to do his share in this task, and on November 2 his first *Examiner* appeared.

The steps outlined above in Swift's so-called conversion to the Tory party have been often rehearsed and sometimes misrepresented. That his alignment with the Harley ministry was eminently to his advantage cannot be denied, but this is hardly sufficient ground for labelling him an apostate or a mercenary. Such an explanation, if nothing else, would be much too simple; "conversions" result usually from a complex of motives, and those which are most obvious are not always most important. Swift's principles, as many scholars have pointed out, remained unchanged; the pamphlets on Church and State discussed in the preceding chapter are compelling evidence of his distaste for the Whig attitude in matters affecting the Church, especially the Sacramental Test.[32] As a Churchman, it was natural for him to gravitate towards the group which seemed most willing to support the Establishment. His action, in other words, was primarily the result of a shift in personal allegiance. The Whig ministers, suspecting his opposition to their efforts for repeal of the Test, had failed for two years to obtain either Swift's own preferment or the benefits which he sought for the Church of Ireland. Harley, whose friendly reception Swift must have contrasted with his rebuff at the hands of Godolphin, had secured the First Fruits only a few weeks after he had been approached. One must not be misled by Swift's obvious pleasure at the flattery and promises of the Tories; in 1708, when Godolphin had sought to barter the First Fruits for political toleration of the dissenters, Swift had refused to compromise his convictions for the sake of expediency. Now he was able to enjoy a personal success with no sacrifice of principle.

But if his sentiments as a Church of England man thus played perhaps the major role in his new political affiliation, there is much to suggest also that his fundamental political notions remained the same, that he did not regard his move as a change from "Whig" to "Tory" principles. Swift was no less vehement than a modern historian like Robert Walcott in deploring the use of those two "fantastick Names." They did not seem to him to bear much relation to the realities of the political situation in which he found himself, or to "those Opinions, which were at first thought to distinguish them." Throughout his life he maintained that he was consistently an "old Whig," or an "angry Whig of the *old* Stamp." In the *Examiner* for March 22, 1710/11, he wrote, "I am not sensible of any material Difference there is between those who call themselves the *Old Whigs,* and a great Majority of the present *Tories."* [33] There is little difference, in other words, between the Whigs of King William's time and the "new Tories" of the Harley administration. This is Swift's claim, and one modern commentator, at least, has accepted it.[34]

What, then, did it mean to be an old Whig? To some extent the term seems to have been honorific, invoked by a variety of groups in much the way that both political parties in this country claim to be "Jeffersonian Democrats." After the accession of the Hanoverians, for example, Bolingbroke, the *Craftsman,* and others in the opposition to Walpole claimed to be old Whigs and asserted that the Walpole administration had adopted the arbitrary principles of the old Toryism. In the earlier period, however, "old Whig" meant opposition to Marlborough and Godolphin and "new Whig" referred specifically to the Junto and their supporters.[35] Even as early as 1701, Charles Davenant had made the charge that modern Whigs were forgetting their original principles, such as opposition to a standing army. It was thus an obvious move for the moderate Harley government in 1710 to claim the support of the "old-principled" Whigs who disliked the measures of the Junto party.[36]

The old principles which the "new Tories" claimed to embody formed a political ideal, an ideal which Swift felt was endangered by the "modern articles and refinements" of the new Whigs. One such principle which Swift certainly accepted was described by Robert Molesworth in an essay written about 1711:

> My Notion of a *Whig,* I mean of a real *Whig* (for the Nominal are worse than any Sort of Men) is, That he is one who is exactly for keeping up to the Strictness of the true old *Gothick Constitution,* under the *Three Estates* of *King* (or *Queen*) *Lords* and *Commons;* the Legislative being seated in all Three together, the *Executive* intrusted with the first, but accomptable to the whole Body of the People, in Case of Male Administration.[37]

Molesworth, writing as an "old Whig," also insisted that a representative in Parliament should be a possessor of land, not a *"monied Man,"* and this again is reiterated throughout Swift's writings. In the so-called *Letter to Mr. Pope* (1720/21) Swift listed both this and certain other tenets which had always

formed the core of his political creed. They included opposition
to a Popish successor to the crown, an antipathy to standing
armies in times of peace, and acceptance of what he calls the
Gothic institution of annual Parliaments. He asserts here, too,
the "Revolution-principle" that a revolution may be justified
when the grievances suffered under a power outweigh the evils
which usually attend a violent change of government.[38]

These, then, are basic political convictions which Swift, in
accordance with a recognized tradition of his time, described as
"old whiggish principles." He did not believe that alliance with
the Harleyite Tories involved any apostasy from this fundamental Whig ideology. On the contrary, "Modern Whigs" like
Addison and Steele might have seemed to him the real apostates.
Their allegiance to the Junto marked them as Whigs with "new
Principles," which Swift professed to "abhor, detest and abjure,
as wholly degenerate from their predecessors." [39] What were the
modern principles which he found so objectionable? For one
thing, the "new whiggery" involved setting up a "monied interest" in opposition to the landed. The support of trade and
the "monied men" by Addison and Steele in the *Spectator* and
elsewhere was obviously a political motif to which Swift would
take violent exception, since he insisted that a preference of the
monied interest to the landed was "dangerous to the Constitution." Moreover, the constant harping on Revolution Principles
by Whig writers also seemed dangerous to Swift, who accepted
the Revolution as sincerely as did Steele, but who accepted it
as a case of extreme necessity. In his view the insistent Whig
advocacy of the doctrine of nonresistance was a rather suspicious
fighting of windmills. Swift would have agreed completely, I
think, with a sermon preached in 1710 by Benjamin Gatton,
who maintained that the practice of resistance has once been
lawful and may be lawful again in cases of the utmost necessity,
but that *"the propagating this Doctrine now with so much Heat
and Violence, is not seasonable, and looks as tho' there were
Designs on Foot which some Men are ashamed to own."* [40] Later,
in the heat of their bitterest political quarrel, Swift was to employ this very argument against Steele.

Finally, the "new Whig" principles of men like Addison and
Steele involved a concept of "party" politics which Swift always

professed to dislike. He deplored the notion that men should "go every length with their party," a notion accepted by Addison and Steele as a fact of political life. He would look cynically at the party loyalty which in 1716 prompted the support of both Addison and Steele for septennial parliaments, an institution characterized by Swift as "directly against the old Whig principles." [41] Swift felt, too, that a dependence on party organization was responsible for that feature of Whiggism which he found most objectionable: their Church policy. To maintain a numerical strength the present Whig party, he says, has been forced to take in people of heterodox opinions in religion and government. He asserts that this is what will always happen in a two-party system; one group will be obliged to woo all the "subaltern Denominations of those who dislike the present Establishment, in order to make themselves a Balance against the other." [42]

The distinction between old Whig principle and new Whig practice thus enabled Swift to justify his agreement to work for the Harley ministry. He could make this move, he felt, without abandoning his basic political ideals, for he had never been a part of the newer Whig tradition represented by his friends Addison and Steele. But the reaction in Whig circles to his shift of allegiance was bitter enough to prove the wisdom of Davenant's character Tom Double, who advised, "Leave off calling thyself an Old Whig, it will do thee hurt with the party." [43]

During these same months when Swift was coming to terms with the new Tory administration, Addison was engaged in preparing to stand for re-election and in contributing to Whig journalism in the present crisis. When his immediate superior, the Earl of Wharton, resigned as Lord Lieutenant on October 13, Addison's duties as Irish Secretary were ended. From September 14 to October 12, he lent his formidable talents as an essayist to the Whig cause by editing and writing the short-lived *Whig-Examiner*. He was probably recruited for this task by Arthur Maynwaring, who may have assisted in the writing of some of the five numbers. Only one of Addison's essays is an actual reply to a specific *Examiner*, and that one defends the Kit-Kat Club and his friend Garth against the criticism of the anonymous Tory journalist. For the most part, Addison directs his attack at St.

John's *Letter to the Examiner,* taking special care to answer that pamphlet's criticism of his friend Steele. He ridicules both St. John's style and his argument, remarking that "there are none of our present Writers who have hit the Sublime in Nonsense, beside Dr. S——*l* in Divinity, and the Author of this Letter in Politicks." Addison's last *Whig-Examiner,* that of October 12, is broader in scope. It states the principal Whig objections to the doctrines of nonresistance and passive obedience, which "are the Duties of *Turks* and *Indians,* who have no Laws above the Will of a *Grand Signior* or a *Mogul.*" [44] It is to the legislative, not the executive body, that the English freeholder must render passive obedience; this, it will be recalled, is essentially the same distinction which Swift had made in *The Sentiments of a Church-of-England Man.* And that he never believed it to be a real issue between the two parties is indicated by this passage, written after his alignment with the Tories:

> This dispute would soon be ended, if the dunces who write on each side, would plainly tell us what the object of this passive obedience is in our country: for, I dare swear, nine in ten of the Whigs will allow it to be the legislature, and as many of the Tories deny it to the Prince alone; and I hardly ever saw a Whig and a Tory together, whom I could not immediately reconcile on that article, when I made them explain themselves. [45]

On this important point of political doctrine, at least, Swift and Addison remained in agreement, although Swift always objected to the constant reiteration of the principle in the Whig press.

After its final paper the *Whig-Examiner* was superseded by Maynwaring's periodical *The Medley,* which was somewhat less urbane than its predecessor had been in rebutting the *Examiner* and consequently perhaps more effective politically. On October 9, Addison's election at Malmesbury passed without opposition. He was now free to devote more time to literary activities, and in the following months he became a regular contributor to the *Tatler.* The fall of his patrons meant that his political aspirations would have to be laid aside, at least temporarily.

Steele's career likewise suffered from the change in ministries, though he apparently made an effort, in part successful, to come to terms with those now in power. A letter of October 9 refers to an unsuccessful attempt to visit Harley, at the request of the minister, and within a week of this date Steele lost the post of Gazetteer. He did not, however, feel it necessary to resign the Stamp Commission until 1713, at which time his letter of resignation implied that in an interview in 1710 Harley had offered him some kind of employment. Furthermore, in a letter to his wife which may have been written about this time, he remarks, "I rejoice that I had spirit to refuse what has been lately offered Me." [46] In Miss Blanchard's opinion, these references show that Steele sought to establish a reasonably friendly relationship with the new ministry; apparently, she points out, he was punished for his support of the Whigs in the *Tatler* by the loss of the Gazetteership and by an order to end the publication of the *Tatler*.[47] In the meantime, he remained a target of the *Examiner,* which on October 12 castigated him as vain and tedious: "He is so intent upon being something Extraordinary, that he scarce knows what he would be."

In retrospect it seems almost inevitable that the political events which had such diverse effects on the fortunes of Steele, Addison, and Swift should have endangered their friendly personal relationship. Nevertheless, while Swift was allowing himself to be courted by the Tories in September and October, the three friends saw a great deal of one another, and Swift made several contributions to the *Tatler*. Smithers takes the frequency of their meetings as "the reflection of doubt and hesitation in Swift's mind before he finally broke with his old associates and cast in his lot with the Tory party." [48] But there is no reason to interpret the situation in this way. Indeed, to meet this often for dinner engagements and the like may not have been at all unusual for the "triumvirate" when they were all in London, since it is only with the beginning of the *Journal to Stella* in September that we have any detailed account of such matters. Moreover, it is unfair to assume, as Smithers does, that Swift himself felt that his association with the Tories would mean the end of his friendship with Addison and Steele. The tenor of all his political writings had been that the concept of "parties" must be kept in proper perspective, that the "Spirit of Faction," if indulged, can destroy "all Ties of Friendship" and break "all the Laws of Charity, Neighbourhood, Alliance and Hospital-

ity." [49] If, however, Swift at this time really expected his cordial
relation with Addison and Steele to remain undisturbed, as
these frequent meetings would seem to indicate, he was soon to
be disillusioned. Even before he took the irrevocable step of
assuming the editorship of the *Examiner,* he was made aware
that his friends resented his new alliances and especially his
efforts to obtain favors for them from the new ministry.

From the very first, Swift indicated his disapproval of Steele's
political activities. Immediately after his arrival in London, he
predicted that "Steele will certainly lose his Gazetteer's place, all
the world detesting his engaging in parties." [50] He was in his
company often in the next few weeks, however, and on September 28 contributed a paper to the *Tatler,* No. 230, concerning
abuses in language and style, a subject which he was later to
treat at length in a letter addressed to Harley. It immediately
follows a clever semipolitical paper by Addison, in which he
answers his critics, including the *Examiner* and the Tory writer
Mrs. Manley, by citing the principle of plenitude: every creature
is the support of "multitudes that are his inferiors," including
"those numberless vermin that feed upon this paper."

In the first few weeks of October Swift continued on cordial
terms with his two friends. He was pleased at Addison's election,
commenting, "I believe, if he had a mind to be chosen king, he
would hardly be refused." [51] On October 14 he reported without
comment that Steele had been deprived of the Gazetteership;
Swift had been receiving his mail at Steele's office and he now
asked that it be sent in care of Addison, at St. James coffeehouse.
Three days later Steele printed Swift's poem "Description of a
City Shower" in *Tatler* No. 238. Ironically, Swift's new contribution to the *Tatler* again appeared in close conjunction with
a political sortie by one of his friends, for in the very next paper,
that of October 19, Addison attacked the *Examiner* in the bitterest of terms. In only two weeks Swift was to be the "scurrilous
wretch" responsible for the Tory journal.

Under the circumstances, these friendly relations could not
continue long, especially when Swift sought to use his new influence with the ministers to help Addison and Steele and was
at a loss to understand why his efforts should provoke so much
resentment in his "cast Whigs." On October 22, he wrote to

Stella of the first open break with the Whig wits. The incident
occurred when Swift, unaware of whatever private arrangement
Steele may have made with Harley, undertook to prevent Steele
from losing his place as Stamp Commissioner. He was encouraged by a government official to "clear matters" with Steele, but
first approached Addison, whose reaction was not at all what
Swift had expected:

> Well, I . . . went to sit with Mr. Addison, and offer the matter at
> distance to him, as the discreeter person; but found *Party* had so
> possessed him, that he talked as if he suspected me, and would not
> fall in with any thing I said. So I stopt short in my overture, and
> we parted very dryly; and I shall say nothing to Steele, and let
> them do as they will; but if things stand as they are, he will cer-
> tainly lose it, unless I save him; and therefore I will not speak to
> him, that I may not report to his disadvantage. . . . When shall
> I grow wise? I endeavour to act in the most exact points of honour
> and conscience, and my nearest friends will not understand it so.
> What must a man expect from his enemies? [52]

Obviously hurt by Addison's resentment at this demonstration
of his standing with the new ministry, Swift behaved "coldly
enough" to his friend the next day. An apology, he felt, was due
him. This particular dispute was apparently quickly settled, at
least on the surface, for Swift in the *Journal* mentions dinner engagements with Addison eight times in the following two weeks
with no indication that the meetings were anything but amicable.
Steele was present on several of these occasions, but it should be
noticed that Swift in these months seems not to have been especially concerned about any rupture of his friendship with Steele.
It was the possibility of an estrangement from Addison which
disturbed him and which he sought to avoid. And despite this
temporary reconciliation in the first weeks of November, he must
have realized that Addison would continue to resent his reception by the political opponents of the Whigs.

On November 2 appeared Swift's first contribution to the *Examiner*. His paper was prefaced by a short section which deserves
to be quoted in full:

> It is a Practice I have generally followed, to converse in equal
> Freedom with the deserving Men of both Parties; and it was never

without some Contempt, that I have observed Persons wholly out of Employment, affect to do otherwise: I doubted whether any Man could owe so much to the side he was of, altho' he were retained by it; but without some great point of Interest, either in Possession or Prospect, I thought it was the Mark of a low and narrow Spirit.

It is hard, that for some Weeks past, I have been forced, in my own Defence, to follow a Proceeding that I have so much condemned in others. But several of my Acquaintance, among the declining Party, are grown so insufferably Peevish and Splenatick, profess such violent Apprehensions for the Publick, and represent the State of Things in such formidable Ideas, that I find myself disposed to share in their Afflictions, although I know them to be groundless and imaginary; or, which is worse, purely affected. To offer them Comfort one by one, would be not only an endless, but a disobliging Task. . . . I shall therefore, instead of hearkning to further Complaints, employ some Part of this Paper for the future, in letting such Men see, that their natural or acquired Fears are ill-grounded, and their artificial ones as ill-intended.[53]

This passage, of course, cannot be read too literally; its purposes are rhetorical, and its tone seeks to create that lofty and judicious air of impartiality which was characteristic of the best political writers. Yet it perhaps has some relevance as well to biographical fact, coming as it does only a few days after the first break in the course of Swift's friendship with Addison and Steele. There is no question, at any rate, that by now they had grown "insufferably Peevish and Splenatick" in Swift's eyes.

One may also accept at face value Swift's expression here of contempt for those who take too seriously the idea of a rigid party loyalty. One of the roots of Swift's difficulty with Addison and Steele at this time certainly lay in the fact that, as we have seen, his conception of the value and function of political parties differed sharply from that of his friends. As officeholders and members of the Kit-Kat Club, they had given allegiance to the Junto and grown accustomed to the support of a specific political group. Even in the early days of his association with them, Swift had not shared their sense of commitment to the Whigs, even though he looked for preferment to his "great friends" in that group. This difference in attitude, which earlier had not affected their personal relations, was now magnified by the current situation. As loyal "new" Whigs, Addison and Steele found Swift's collaboration with the Harley ministry intolerable; Swift, skeptical of the validity of party ties, was hurt that their friendship for him should be affected "by this damned business of party."

In November and December Swift saw very little of Addison. Their relationship had settled into a less intimate and rather formal pattern: "Mr. Addison and I meet a little seldomer than formerly, although we are still at bottom as good friends as ever; but differ a little about party." So wrote Swift on November 16; a few weeks later he comments that he and Addison hardly meet once a fortnight: "His Parliament and my different friendships keep us asunder." They dined together on December 14, however, and the occasion prompted Swift to analyze for Stella the change in their relationship. Remarking that they were now as "different as black and white," he places the blame for the situation on their political differences: "He cannot bear seeing me fall in so with this ministry; but I love him still as well as ever, though we seldom meet." [54]

It is hardly surprising that Swift should have ceased contributing to the *Tatler* in these months. To Stella he wrote that he would no longer supply Steele with material, coupling this resolution with a few resentful remarks about his former friend:

> We have scurvy *Tatlers* of late: so pray do not suspect me. I have one or two hints I design to send him, and never any more: he does not deserve it. He is governed by his wife most abominably, as bad as —— I never saw her since I came; nor has he ever made me an invitation.[55]

One of the hints which he supplied was used by Addison on November 11, in *Tatler* No. 249, which detailed the history of a shilling. In his introductory remarks, Addison gives credit for the idea to a "friend of mine who has an inexhaustible fund of discourse." Writing to Stella a month later, Swift admits that the suggestion was his, but adds that he has been reproached by his friends in the ministry for helping Steele and that he has agreed to do so no longer. As far as is known, Swift kept this resolution; none of the remaining *Tatlers* can be connected with him, although Stella apparently insisted on identifying various essays as his.

It may be noted, however, that on December 2 a letter partly by Swift did appear in *Tatler* No. 258. Steele, in an earlier number, had sought to encourage the use of the term "British" in place of "English." The letter, by Swift, Rowe, and Prior, reduces the "new style" to absurdity: "So we paid our North Briton sooner than we designed, and took coach to North Britain Yard, about which place most of us live." [56] Swift's account of the incident follows:

> Steele, the rogue, has done the impudentest thing in the world; he said something in a *Tatler,* that we ought to use the word Great Britain, and not England, in common conversation. . . . Upon this Rowe, Prior, and I sent him a letter, turning this into ridicule. He has to-day printed the letter, and signed it J. S. M. P. and N. R. the first letters of all our names.[57]

There is a political touch to this exchange, involving the Whig and Tory attitudes toward the Union, but the tone is light and playful, surprisingly so for this stage of Swift's relations with Steele.

As bad as these relations were, they would have become immeasurably worse if Steele and Addison had recognized Swift's hand in the *Examiners* which appeared in November and December. As Herbert Davis points out, one of Swift's primary functions in the early *Examiners* was to justify the change in ministry, a task which necessarily involved discrediting the members of the Junto.[58] Those attacked inevitably included men for whom Addison and Steele felt a deep respect and loyalty. In No. 16, for November 23, Swift began this campaign with a paper on Marlborough. The relations of the new ministry with the Duke were still rather ambiguous, and Swift does not attack him directly. His essay is in the form of a reply to charges in the Whig press that the nation had been ungrateful to the victorious general, the ingratitude, according to Swift, consisting in a change of government while the Duke was abroad. Swift maintains that only respect for Marlborough had prevented an even earlier defeat for the Junto, with whom the Duke was joined "by Friendship, Interest, Alliance, Inclination and Opinion." [59] He then enumerates the substantial rewards which Marlborough had received, comparing them favorably with those of a victorious

Roman general. Swift's emphasis on the *material* compensation granted to Marlborough is a subtle suggestion of the charge against the Duke which he expressed privately and which he was to develop for the public the following year: "He is covetous as Hell, and ambitious as the Prince of it." Swift's paper is discreet enough, but it could hardly have failed to arouse the indignation of Addison, author of the *Campaign,* or, especially, of Steele, who gave to Marlborough "one of the great loyalties" of his life.[60] Their friend Maynwaring, in the *Medley* for December 4, attacked this issue of the *Examiner* as "the falsest Paper that ever was printed."

In the next year and a half Marlborough was to become the center of a furious pamphlet warfare and the source of much of the difficulty between Swift and Steele. Perhaps, then, some general comment on his role might be appropriate at this point. Obviously, Steele's lavish praise and Swift's satiric portraits both represent extreme points of view. Marlborough was neither a demigod nor a corrupt warmonger, but an extraordinary leader whose successes placed him in a crucial political position. At first the new ministers wished to pacify the General, to keep him in the field so that they could secure a more advantageous peace. When the time came, as it did late in 1711, that Marlborough rallied the Allies and spoke in the House of Lords against the preliminary terms of the peace, the ministry no longer had reason to deal gently with him. The flood of propaganda against him both before and after his dismissal in December of 1711 was an essential step in achieving the Tory peace.

Thus the campaign against Marlborough was not simply shameful mistreatment of a great national hero, as Whigs like Steele would have us believe. Their indignation cannot be taken at face value, any more than the Tory abuse can. The fact is that Marlborough was not only a deservedly popular idol but also a political power in the Whig opposition; and the government sought to turn popular opinion against him in the accustomed manner of the day. Though we would not learn it from reading Steele, there were very real limitations to the Duke's character which could be exploited in a propaganda attack: his love of money, his request to be made Captain-General for life, his passion for the building of Blenheim as a monument to his fame, and so on. In the hands of government writers like Swift, such foibles could be exaggerated and distorted into the image required for public consumption. In *Examiner* No. 16, Swift is filling in the first detail of this image. Both his later attacks and Steele's defenses must be read as partisan exaggerations, motivated perhaps by sincere personal conviction but certainly by political necessity.

In the following issue of the *Examiner* Swift makes a considerably harsher attack on the Whig leader whom he despised the most, the Earl of Wharton. His method here, as he himself candidly explains, is to make use of an historical figure resembling the target of his attack. In this case he employs an "abstract" from Cicero's orations against Verres, the notorious governor of Sicily. First, however, he makes this comment:

> I remember a younger Brother of mine, who deceased about two Months ago, presented the World with a Speech of *Alcibiades*, against an *Athenian* Brewer: Now, I am told for certain, that in those Days there was no Ale in *Athens;* and therefore that Speech, or at least, a great Part of it, must needs be spurious. The Difference between me and my Brother is this; he makes *Alcibiades* say a great deal more than he really did; and I make *Cicero* say a great deal less.[61]

The reference is to Addison's *Whig-Examiner* No. 3 (September 28), where the parody of Alcibiades is made to support the election of General Stanhope, opposed by a brewer. Thus, by a curious irony, Swift points up his use of Addison's device, which in his hands becomes a vehicle for attacking the member of the Junto who a few months before had been Addison's immediate political superior. (The irony may be intentional; there is no way of determining whether Swift knew of Addison's authorship of the *Whig-Examiner.*) The attack itself is extremely severe, reflecting Swift's personal animosity for Wharton and making liberal use of the Earl's wide reputation as a rake. The *Medley* attempted, rather ineffectively, to answer Swift's invective by giving evidence that Wharton's had been a popular government in Ireland.

In December Swift continued his campaign against Wharton by publishing *A Short Character of His Ex. T. E. of W.* It is

one of the most violent of his political tracts, although, para-
doxically, the force of the personal invective arises from its appearance of calm impersonality. Swift begins with an ironic denial that Wharton's "person" is the object of his attack. His essay
cannot be considered a personal attack, he explains, for Wharton
is both indifferent to applause and "insensible of Reproach."
He is, in fact, "without the Sense of Shame or Glory, as some
Men are without the Sense of Smelling." [62] And Swift himself
neither loves nor hates Wharton, he tells us, just as one who
describes the nature of a wolf or a serpent "must be understood
to do it without any personal Love or Hatred for the Animals
themselves." By establishing as his premise this insensibility to
ordinary human values, which is a "meer unaffected Bent" of
Wharton's nature, Swift is able to sketch his portrait with an
air of complete detachment. His tone is impersonal and dispassionate, as he analyzes such elements in Wharton's character
as these:

> He sweareth solemnly he loveth, and will serve you; and your
> Back is no sooner turned, but he tells those about him you are a
> Dog and a Rascal. He goeth constantly to Prayers in the Forms of
> his Place, and will talk Bawdy and Blasphemy at the Chapel Door.
> He is a Presbyterian in Politics, and an Atheist in Religion; but he
> chuseth at present to whore with a Papist.[63]

After completing an account of "his Excellency's Merits," Swift
describes several examples of Wharton's misgovernment; the
Short Character is then supplemented by *A Relation of Several
Facts* concerning Wharton's behavior in Ireland, which apparently Swift did not write.

Once again, there is no evidence that Addison or Steele suspected Swift's authorship of this pamphlet, and it is consequently
pointless to speculate on the immediate effect which it might
have had on their personal relations. It serves, however, as a
further illustration of the distance which now separated the three
men in their attitudes toward public figures and events. Steele,
as Miss Blanchard points out, had a "genuine admiration" for
Wharton, who to some extent directed his political career; he had
praised the Earl in the *Tatler,* and in 1713 he dedicated to

Wharton the fifth volume of the *Spectator*, making reference to his "Generous Designs for the Publick Good." [64] Addison, of course, had played an important role in the Irish administration which Swift attacks, consistently supporting the policies of the Lord Lieutenant; and he was under personal obligation to Wharton for the success of his election in Malmesbury. Nowhere does he make any unfavorable comments about Wharton's character. In his only reference to Swift's *Short Character*, he calls it simply "ye scurrilous little Book." [65]

These attacks on Marlborough and Wharton are perhaps less important as a factor in the collapse of Swift's friendship with Addison and Steele than his continued efforts to gain patronage for them. The situation was now the reverse of what it had been only six months earlier; Swift was now in a position to act as a "great friend" for some of those who had earlier sought to use political influence to help him in his own preferment. His efforts, however, seemed to his Whig friends merely to underscore the abrupt reversal of positions and increased their bitterness at his defection. In *Examiner* No. 18 (December 7) Swift comments on his solicitations in behalf of Whig writers:

> A certain starveling Author who *worked* under the late Administration, told me with a heavy Heart, above a Month ago, That he and some others of his Brethren, had secretly offered their Service dog-cheap to the present Ministry; but were all refused. . . . I have been of late employed out of perfect Commiseration, in doing them good Offices: For, whereas some were of Opinion that these hungry Zealots should not be suffered any longer in their malapert Way to snarl at the present Course of publick Proceedings; . . . I humbly gave my Advice, that they should be suffered to write on, as they used to do; which I did purely out of Regard to their Persons: For I hoped it would keep them out of Harms-way. . . . [66]

It would be absurd to read such a passage literally, but it is likely that once again Swift has exaggerated and distorted an actual situation for the purposes of propaganda. For at this same time he was again attempting to intercede with the ministry in behalf of Steele, who, he believed, was still in danger of losing his post of Stamp Commissioner. He writes to Stella of Steele's failure to keep an appointment with Harley which Swift had secured for him:

> Whether it was blundering, sullenness, insolence, or rancor of party, I cannot tell; but I shall trouble myself no more about him. I believe Addison hindered him out of meer spight, being grated to the soul to think he should ever want my help to save his friend; yet now he is soliciting me to make another of his friends queen's secretary at Geneva; and I'll do it if I can, it is poor Pastoral Philips.[67]

Still unaware of whatever private agreement Steele had come to with Harley, Swift can only feel contempt for what he considers Steele's ingratitude. He assumes, here and elsewhere, that Steele owed his original appointment as Gazetteer to Harley, although in all probability this was not the case.[68] Nonetheless, he was willing to use his influence with the ministry to help another of his former friends among the Whig wits, "poor Pastoral Philips." That his intercession was both solicited and at the same time resented is indicated by a letter from Addison to Philips:

> You know very well that all my great friends are entirely out of favour. I have spoken to Dr. Swift (who is much caressed and invited almost every day to dinner by some or other of the new ministry) to recommend the affair either to Mr. Harley or Mr. St. John, which I verily believe might be effectual; and he has given me a kind of promise if he finds a favourable opportunity. I fancy if you writ such a letter to the Dr. as he might produce on occasion, it would not be amiss. . . .[69]

Philips at this time was in Copenhagen, as secretary to the British envoy; Swift's efforts in his behalf were to no avail, for the post in Geneva was discontinued. In the next few years Swift was to make similar recommendations in behalf of Philips and other Whig writers. He was proud of this activity, and much later, in 1721, he wrote that "it was in those times a usual subject of raillery towards me among the Ministers, that I never came to them without a Whig in my sleeve." [70] He was puzzled (or he professed to be puzzled) that Addison should be "grated to the soul" at his offers of help. Although they were willing enough to accept whatever aid he could give them, it is clear from Swift's comments and Addison's letter that his Whig friends deeply re-

sented his offers to obtain patronage for them and that this resentment contributed to the disintegration of his friendships
among the Whigs in the winter of 1710/11.

On January 2 Steele published his last number of the *Tatler*,
signed for the first time with his own name. There is some reason
to believe that "he lay'd it down as a sort of Submission to, and
Composition with the Government for some past Offences," as
John Gay suggested a few months later.[71] However, in the course
of his farewell paper, Steele makes no apologies for his occasional
excursions into politics but defends them on the ground that
public duty has compelled him to touch on matters of Church
and State. Swift, incidentally, assumed that the end of the *Tatler*
was the natural result of Steele's literary incompetence. The
paper, he wrote Stella, had grown very dull, and though Steele
had been furnished with several good hints, he had been too
lazy to make proper use of them. The "hints," no doubt, were
those which Swift himself had supplied.

The *Tatler*, with its transmutation of Swift's "Bickerstaff" to
Steele's, had first appeared when the ties of friendship and
mutual esteem among the "triumvirate" were most strong, and
its demise now in January of 1710/11 coincided with the end of
that cordial relationship. Two weeks after Steele's final paper,
Swift made this comment about Addison:

> . . . all our friendship and dearness are off: we are civil acquaint-
> ance, talk words of course, of when we shall meet, and that's all.
> I have not been at any house with him these six weeks: . . . Is not
> it odd? But I think he has used me ill, and I have used him too
> well, at least his friend Steele.[72]

The period of transition was over; there was no longer any
reason to hope that this particular friendship could survive the
destructive effects of partisan politics.

3

THE YEARS OF THE
SPECTATOR

Y THE END of the *Tatler* political differences had thus produced a rift in Swift's friendship with Addison and Steele; by
the end of the *Spectator,* two years later, the rift had widened
immeasurably. In the period which will now be surveyed party
lines hardened, and Swift emerged as the leading propagandist
in the Tory efforts to conclude a peace. His authorship of the
Examiner and of such influential pamphlets as *The Conduct of
the Allies* increased the hostility with which the Whig writers
regarded him, and his participation in the ministry's campaign
to discredit the Duke of Marlborough became a special source
of ill feeling. Though Swift on one occasion joined in an attack
on the *Spectator,* he and Steele were not yet open antagonists;
but each new political issue made increasingly clear their conflicting loyalties and interests.

1.

One minor and rather amusing squabble between Swift and
Steele, just as the *Spectator* was getting under way, was actually

not political but literary. Swift had recently undertaken the guidance of a young Whig writer named William Harrison, and with the aid of St. John he now sponsored Harrison in a continuation of the *Tatler*. Swift contributed several essays to this journal, which ran from January 13 to May 19, 1711, and revised a few more; but he had a poor opinion of Harrison's ability to emulate Steele: "I am afraid the little toad has not the true vein for it." [1] Naturally, this enterprise brought Swift and Harrison into conflict not only with two or three rival continuations but with Steele himself. In his first number, which had been approved by Swift, Harrison pretends that he is the genuine author of the *Tatler* and that during a brief absence from town Richard Steele, an impostor, has played a joke on him by signing a farewell paper with his name. He prints a letter from "Humphrey Wagstaff," the pseudonym Swift had used in contributing his two poems to the *Tatler,* which expresses surprise that Steele, "a Man of Wit and Honour," should attempt to "perswade the Town that there was some Analogy between *Isaac Bickerstaff* and him." [2] He continued in this vein in the second issue, with references to "Mr. S—le, the pretended TATLER from *Morphew*." With the beginning of the *Spectator* in March, Harrison again attacked Steele, accusing the new venture of being a "party" paper and even complaining that Addison and Steele have hired men to steal copies of the *Tatler* and replace them with *Spectators*.[3] But in the *Tatler* for March 24, for which Swift was responsible to some extent, Steele receives better treatment. The purpose of the paper is to trace the many forms which have been assumed by the soul of Isaac Bickerstaff, and Hilario (Steele) is praised as a writer of wit and insight. A few issues later, however, Harrison again carps at Steele: "Let *Hilario* be pleasant, and let some of his Friends have Wit; But does it naturally follow from thence that he is a Philosopher?" Swift's share in Harrison's continuation was well known, and, as Professor Robert Elliott points out, "bickering of this kind must have contributed to the estrangement between Steele and Swift." [4]

In the meantime Swift was almost completely occupied in this spring of 1711 by the composition of the *Examiners*. His purpose at the moment in these papers was both to discredit the

Whig ministers and their associates and to show that the new govenment embodied moderate principles which "Whigs" as well as "Tories" could accept. The effectiveness of his propaganda is perhaps indicated by the violent reaction to the *Examiner* in such Whig journals as the *Medley,* although it was apparently not until late spring that the Whigs, including Addison and Steele, were aware that Swift was the writer they were attacking so abusively. It was Swift's disparagement of the individual political leaders of the late ministry that especially infuriated the Whigs. In No. 27 for February 8, for example, he once more attacked Steele's idol, the Duke of Marlborough, this time somewhat more severely than he had in the past. Beginning with a general discussion of avarice in the traditional manner of moralists, he makes the personal application in the form of a letter to "Marcus Crassus," a member of the first Roman triumvirate. He is careful not to impugn Marlborough's military skill, freely admitting that Crassus is *"a most successful General, of long Experience, great Conduct, and much Personal Courage."* Nevertheless, he is *"deeply stained with that odious and ignoble Vice of* Covetousness," and Swift calls upon him to quit this vice and become a *"truly Great Man."* [5] Swift apparently felt that such charges against the Duke, whom in some respects he admired, were fully justified. To the Whig writers, however, an attack on Marlborough represented the ultimate sin; the *Medley's* answer to this issue of the *Examiner* is frenetically abusive.

On the other hand, Swift reported that he was taxed by some for being too gentle with the Duke, a circumstance which again supports his claim that in the *Examiner* he represented a moderate position between the extremes of the two parties. In his paper for February 15, a belated answer to St. John's *Letter to the Examiner,* he speaks of the difficulty of maintaining this position and prints a letter from a Whig and one from a Tory, each attacking him as an extremist. Part of his task in the *Examiner* was to defend the ministry by defining from his moderate point of view terms which had become party issues, such as "passive obedience." And one of his last papers for the *Examiner,* No. 43 for May 31, ridicules those "two fantastick Names of *Whig* and *Tory,*" which no longer have any relation to actual principles. The tenets originally held by both those groups, he asserts, are now accepted by "a great Majority of the Kingdom" (that is, by the supporters of the Harley government). These principles include those once thought of as "Whig," such as belief in the limited monarchy, the Revolution Settlement, and the Hanoverian Succession, and such "Tory" opinions as these:

> . . . that the Persons of Princes were Sacred; their lawful Authority not to be resisted on any Pretence; nor even their Usurpations, without the most extream Necessity: That, Breaches in the Succession were highly dangerous; that, *Schism* was a great Evil, both in it self and its Consequences; that, the Ruin of the *Church,* would probably be attended with that of the *State;* that, no Power should be trusted with those who are not of the established Religion. . . .[6]

Consequently, modern Whigs, for Swift, are those linked to a "certain Sett of *Persons*" rather than any set of principles, and he defines a member of that party as "one *who believed in the late Ministry.*" Obviously, this argument has relevance to Swift's personal situation; as we have observed, he was anxious that his alliance with the Harley ministry be recognized as a shift in personal allegiance, not in principles. At the beginning of this spring, on February 28, he had finally published his *Miscellanies in Prose and Verse,* without the preface by Steele originally planned, and he clearly hoped that the pamphlets on Church and State which it contained would demonstrate his political consistency. Thus, the Advertisement to the *Letter concerning the Sacramental Test* assures the reader that it is no disadvantage to the author for this piece to be revived in 1711, "considering the Time when it was Writ, the Persons then at the Helm, and the Designs in Agitation, against which this Paper so boldly appeared." [7]

At one point during Swift's authorship of the *Examiner,* Steele became his journalistic opponent by writing an essay for the *Medley,* No. 23 (March 5, 1710/11). Swift had defended his attack on Marlborough in the "Letter to Crassus" as merely friendly advice; to reprove the Duke for his avarice is analogous, he wrote, to pointing out smut on the face of a "handsome young Fellow going to a Ball at Court." Steele retorted with the story of a ball at Wapping, attended by sailors and colliers. The colliers, discovering that the sailors are dressed in their best clothes,

retire to wash themselves. But their leader advises them simply
to jostle the sailors so as to make them as black as the colliers
themselves. This, continues Steele, is the case of the *Examiner,*
a "Reviver of confuted Calumnies, who has no regard to the
Dictates of Truth, nor even the Sentiments of common Humanity." [8]

Steele may very well have written these words without realizing that the object of his abuse was his former friend, Jonathan
Swift. There was still no hint that the identity of the Tory
writer was known to Maynwaring or his associates on the *Medley,*
despite several dark innuendoes or such vague disparagement as,
"No Man of Common Sense ever thought any body wrote the
Paper but *Abel Roper,* or some of his Allies." [9] As late as May
28, the *Medley* had still failed to connect Swift with the *Examiner,* for in its issue of that date it accused the Tory writer of
blasphemy without mentioning *A Tale of a Tub,* a move which
would have been obvious had Swift's authorship of the *Examiner*
been known. The omission of any reference to Swift at that late
date is curious, since Gay's *The Present State of Wit,* which also
appeared in May, reports that Swift is the reputed author of
the paper. It is only as a comment on Swift's last paper that the
Medley, in No. 38 for June 18, finally hints of his part in the
Examiner, and it is interesting that in the same issue Swift is
accused of imitating Steele by copying an old joke used by the
Tatler. The *Examiner* had made reference to a Whig writer as
a Non-Juror, and it is in the answer to that remark that the
allusion to Swift is introduced:

> And if he talks of him merely as an Author, all the Authors in
> the World are Nonjurors, but the ingenious Divine who writ *the
> Tale of a Tub.* He, I say, is the only Writer in the World who is
> not a Nonjuror; for he is the first Man who introduc'd those
> Figures of Rhetorick we call Swearing and Cursing in Print.[10]

Shortly after Swift's last contribution, however, the *Medley* un-
intentionally complimented him by remarking of the new papers
by Mrs. Manley, "The *Examiner* is grown so insipid and contemptible, that my Acquaintance are offended at my troubling
my self about him." On July 26, 1711, the *Examiner* temporarily
ceased publication, and the *Medley* soon followed suit.

Addison and Steele were now occupied by the *Spectator,* which had begun on March 1. Swift had taken note of their new venture in his *Journal,* both praising the quality of the papers and renewing his resolution to break all ties with the Whig writers:

> Have you seen the *Spectator* yet, a paper that comes out every day? 'Tis written by Mr. Steele, who seems to have gathered new life, and have a new fund of wit; it is in the same nature as his *Tatlers,* and they have all of them had something pretty. I believe Addison and he club. I never see them; and I plainly told Mr. Harley and Mr. St. John, ten days ago, before my lord keeper and lord Rivers, that I had been foolish enough to spend my credit with them in favour of Addison and Steele; but that I would engage and promise never to say one word in their behalf, having been used so ill for what I had already done.[11]

As far as is known, Swift made no contribution to the *Spectator,* although one issue, No. 50, is based on a suggestion he had originally made for use in the *Tatler.* This is the essay by Addison describing a visit of four Indian kings to England; their supposed reaction to various aspects of English life serves as a vehicle for satire on manners. For example, one of the kings comments about St. Paul's, "It is probable that when this great work was begun, which must have been many hundred years ago, there was some religion among this people." [12] Addison also takes occasion here to satirize party politics; the chiefs are warned to avoid monsters called Whigs, who would knock them down for being kings, and animals called Tories, who would treat them as badly for being foreigners. All of this is very much in the manner of Swift, who expressed his irritation at the essay to Stella:

> The *Spectator* is written by Steele, with Addison's help: 'tis often very pretty. Yesterday it was made of a noble hint I gave him long ago for his *Tatlers,* about an Indian supposed to write his travels into England. I repent he ever had it. I intended to have written a book on that subject. I believe he has spent it all in one paper, and all the under-hints there are mine too; but I never see him or Addison.[13]

None of the other *Spectators* can be connected with Swift in any way. He was content to remain aloof from the astonishing literary success achieved by Addison and Steele, and he was not to be mollified by such occasional complimentary allusions to him in the pages of that periodical as "a late ingenious author" or "one of the greatest geniuses this age has produced." Swift was unimpressed by such recognition from Addison and Steele and unconcerned about the subjects of their light satire: "I will not meddle with the Spectator, let him fair-sex it to the world's end." [14]

Some of Swift's irritation was doubtless caused by the Whiggish cast of the *Spectator*. In May, John Gay's *Present State of Wit,* though professing to be politically impartial, extended such praise to Addison and Steele that his criticism was marked as that of one close to the Whigs. Swift, in fact, suspected that the Whig writers themselves were responsible for the pamphlet:

> The author seems to be a Whig, yet he speaks very highly of a paper called the *Examiner,* and says the supposed author of it is Dr. Swift. But above all things he praises the *Tatlers* and *Spectators;* and I believe Steele and Addison were privy to the printing of it. Thus is one treated by these impudent dogs.[15]

In his pamphlet Gay expresses his hope that Addison's "known Temper and Prudence" will restrain Steele from "ever lashing out into Party." In effect, something of the sort seems to have taken place, for the *Spectator* was seldom as openly partisan as the *Tatler* had been. Its campaign in behalf of the Whigs was subtle, conducted by implication rather than overt argument. The volumes of the collected edition were all dedicated to Whig leaders, and contemporary readers would not have missed the invidious description of a Tory squire, the praise of the Duke of Marlborough, or the other Whig motifs which regularly appeared in its pages.[16]

While Addison and Steele, whose party was out of power, thus chose to be circumspect in their approach to political matters, Swift continued his activities in support of the ministry unhampered by any fear of government reprisal. He had ended his work as *Examiner* in June and was free to serve the government during the remainder of 1711 by writing a number of political pamphlets. Not all of these need be discussed here in detail. They included *Some Remarks upon a Pamphlet Entitled*

A Letter to the Seven Lords, in which the "Examiner" attacks Whig efforts to use the Greg affair of 1708 as a weapon against Harley, and *A New Journey to Paris,* the purpose of which was to mislead the public about the nature of Prior's negotiations for peace with the French. But by far Swift's most significant piece of propaganda was *The Conduct of the Allies and of the Late Ministry in Beginning and Carrying on the Present War,* which was timed to appear at the opening of Parliament in November. Here Swift's purpose is to state the case for the kind of peace the ministry was negotiating with France. All good Whigs, such as Addison and Steele, were crying "No Peace without Spain." Swift reminds his readers that the original goals of the Allies in the war had not included the expulsion of the Bourbon Philip from Spain as a condition of any peace, only that France and Spain never be united under the same king. He argues powerfully that England has borne the brunt of a war which she should never have entered as a principal, that the Allies are receiving the profit at England's expense, and that despite a series of victories the war has been carried on in areas where opposition was strongest and where England could receive the least advantages. He lays the blame for this situation on the Duke of Marlborough and those allied with him in the Whig ministry, and on the monied interests; it was begun, he says, as "a War of the *General* and the *Ministry,* and not of the *Prince* or *People*." [17] All of this, of course, was calculated to turn public opinion against the Allies, especially Holland, and justify Harley's negotiations with France: "We who bore the Burthen of the War, ought, in reason, to have the greatest share in making the Peace." The success of *The Conduct of the Allies* was prodigious, Swift reporting at the end of January that it had sold eleven thousand copies. In Trevelyan's opinion, it "materially helped" to bring peace to Europe.[18] But it provoked an onslaught from the Whig press, which immediately recognized Swift's hand and was quick to accuse him of apostasy, of having served as the *"Buffoon of One Party"* and become the *"Setting Dog* of Another." [19]

Very obviously, Swift's authorship of such tracts in 1711 necessarily increased the hostility with which Steele and Addison regarded him because of his political activities, but he no longer expressed much regret about the estrangement. "All our friendship is over," he wrote in March, 1711, and the following month he instructed Archbishop King to direct his mail to Erasmus Lewis instead of to Addison. Swift by this time had been welcomed by a new circle of friends, composed of some of the leading members of the ministry. Although occasionally he would receive an invitation from one of his former associates among the Whigs, such as Anthony Henley, he was much more gratified by his admission into the company of Harley, St. John, Harcourt, or Prior. To Stella he described with some pleasure his change of company:

> Prithee, don't you observe how strangely I have changed my company and manner of living? I never go a Coffee-house; you hear no more of Addison, Steele, Henley, lady Lucy, Mrs. Finch, lord Somers, lord Hallifax, &c. I think I have altered for the better.[20]

In place of this Whig circle of the coffeehouses, Swift turned eagerly to such Tory groups as the Saturday Club, originally an informal conference on political strategy attended by Harley, St. John, and Harcourt, and "The Society" or "Brothers Club," as it is generally known. The latter group, formed in June of 1711, included leading members of the ministry, though not Harley, and "men of wit," such as Swift, Prior, and Arbuthnot. St. John, who was the dominating figure of the club, expressed its purpose as "the improvement of friendship, and the encouragement of letters." [21] In effect, of course, it was to be the Tory rival of the Whig Kit-Kat Club.

Swift's alienation from the Whig wits, then, by no means resulted in social isolation. He and his former friends now moved in different worlds, and if there was as yet no open hostility between them, Swift was fairly unconcerned about his lack of contact with Addison and Steele in 1711. Their personal relations were so strained at this time that it is really curious to find Steele paying Swift a compliment in the preface to the fourth volume of the *Tatler,* which appeared on April 17, dedicated to Halifax. There he again confesses his indebtedness to Swift for his share in the early *Tatler:*

> I have in the dedication of the first volume made my acknowledgments to Dr. Swift, whose pleasant writings, in the name of Bickerstaff, created an inclination in the town towards anything

that could appear in the same disguise. I must acknowledge also, that at my first entering upon this work, a certain uncommon way of thinking, and a turn in conversation peculiar to that agreeable gentleman, rendered his company very advantageous to one whose imagination was to be continually employed upon obvious and common subjects, though at the same time obliged to treat of them in a new and unbeaten method.[22]

Steele then praises the two poems which Swift had contributed. As far as is known, Swift did not acknowledge this compliment. Perhaps at this juncture he was not entirely pleased to have the public reminded of his connection with the *Tatler*.[23]

The issue of patronage continued to cause difficulties in 1711 between Swift and the Whig writers, but in a manner slightly different from that of the incidents of the preceding autumn. The root of the trouble was no longer their resentment at Swift's offers of help, for by this time he was simply unwilling to use his influence with the ministry to help former friends who solicited his aid. In June, for example, Steele, in a letter which has not been preserved, requested Swift's intervention on behalf of a friend. Swift's reaction was unfavorable:

Steele has had the assurance to write to me, that I would engage my lord treasurer to keep a friend of his in an employment: I believe I told you how he and Addison served me for my good offices in Steele's behalf; and I promised lord treasurer never to speak for either of them again.

In reply, he sent Steele a "biting letter." The very next day Swift resolved not to help Philips, who was continuing his search for employment:

This evening I have had a letter from Mr. Phillips the pastoral poet, to get him a certain employment from lord treasurer. I have now had almost all the Whig poets my solicitors; and I have been useful to Congreve, Steele, and Harrison; but I will do nothing for Phillips; I find he is more a puppy than ever; so don't solicit for him. Besides, I will not trouble lord treasurer, unless upon some very extraordinary occasion.[24]

Such an attitude, of course, was not likely to ease the tension between Swift and the group of "Whig poets."

There were occasional meetings, nonetheless, and much deploring of excessive partisanship as a destructive element in personal relations. Addison, in *Spectator* No. 125 (July 24, 1711), discusses the damage done by a "furious party-spirit." He begins with a reflection by Sir Roger against parties, "how they spoil good neighbourhood, and make honest gentlemen hate one another: besides that they manifestly tend to the prejudice of the Land Tax, and the destruction of the game." [25] After this jibe of his own at a Tory squire, Addison protests that because of political differences many men are becoming alienated from one another in a manner "altogether inconsistent with the dictates of either reason or religion." He then attacks political pamphleteering and the calumny so often involved in political writing, and calls for a neutral association in which men of merit will regard one another as friends regardless of political affiliation. Two days after the appearance of this essay, on July 26, Swift finally met once more with Addison and Steele, at the home of Jacob Tonson. Swift describes the meeting as rather friendly:

> Mr. Addison and I have at last met again. I dined with him and Steele to-day at young Jacob Tonson's. . . . Mr. Addison and I talked as usual, and as if we had seen one another yesterday; and Steele and I were very easy, although I writ him lately a biting letter, in answer to one of his, where he desired me to recommend a friend of his to lord treasurer.[26]

In September he recorded another meeting with Addison, this time in the company of Philips: "We were very good company; and yet know no man half so agreeable to me as he is."

2.

Despite such occasional *rapprochements,* the political events of the winter of 1711/12 could only have deepened the ill feeling between Swift and the leading figures of the Whig literary world. A crisis in the Tory campaign for peace occurred at the opening of Parliament in November, when the House of Lords voted an amendment to the Queen's Address, resolving against a Peace without Spain. This action, disastrous to the interests of Swift and his friends, was taken on the motion of the Tory Earl of Nottingham, who in return for this service to the Whig Lords gained their support for his Occasional Conformity Bill. Because of his amendment, which was supported by Marlborough, Nottingham was severely attacked by the Tories, who considered him a turncoat. Swift wrote *An Excellent New Song, Being the Intended Speech of a famous Orator against Peace,* which opens:

> An Orator *dismal* of *Nottinghamshire*
> Who has forty Years let out his Conscience to hire,
> Out of Zeal for his Country, and *want of a Place,*
> Is come up, *vi & armis,* to *break the Q*—'s *Peace.*[27]

To Swift and many others it seemed that the Harley ministry was doomed to fall, despite the fact that popular support for the peace was growing, as indicated by the success of *The Conduct of the Allies.* But the Queen remained loyal to her ministers; on December 31, Marlborough was dismissed from his command and the following day twelve new peers were created, giving the Tories a majority in the House of Lords. Swift wrote to Stella, "I have broke open my letter, and tore it into the bargain; to let you know, that we are all safe. . . ."[28]

During this period of political tension, it was inevitable that Swift's activities in support of the ministry should come into direct conflict with those of Steele and Addison. One relatively minor incident will serve to illustrate the manner in which political affairs this winter acted as a further irritant in the strained relations between the Tory propagandist and the members of the Kit-Kat Club. On November 17, 1711, the anniversary of the accession of Queen Elizabeth, a procession of the sort customarily staged by apprentices was planned by the Whigs. Effigies of the Pope, the Pretender, fourteen cardinals and fourteen devils, monks, Jesuits, and similar personages were to be carried through London and burnt before the statue of Queen Elizabeth. The procession was to be closed by twenty streamers, on each of which was written, "God bless Queen *Anne,* the nation's great defender! / Keep out the *French,* the Pope, and the Pretender."[29] The government, however, confiscated the images from a house in Drury Lane and so prevented the celebration from taking place. Swift's account of the incident follows:

> This is queen Elizabeth's birth-day, usually kept in this town by 'prentices, &c. but the Whigs designed a mighty procession by midnight, and had laid out a thousand pounds to dress up the Pope,

Devil, Cardinals, Sacheverell, &c. and carry them with torches about, and burn them. They did it by contribution. Garth gave five guineas. . . . But they were seized last night, by order from the secretary. . . . They had some very foolish and mischievous designs; and it was thought they would have put the rabble upon assaulting my lord treasurer's house, and the secretary's; and other violences. The Militia was raised to prevent it, and now, I suppose, all will be quiet.[30]

It was also rumored that the Devil had been made to look as much like Harley as possible; but Swift reported after seeing the images that such was not the case and that his account of the money involved had also been exaggerated.

The date of this procession was coincident with the arrival of the Duke of Marlborough in England. The Tories, consequently, spread the report that there was a "deeper Meaning" to the affair than a mere political demonstration, that, in fact, the Duke intended to place himself at the head of the mob. Swift later made this insinuation in his account of the incident in his *History of the Last Four Years of the Queen,* concluding with the ominous remark, "And if what was confidently affirmed be true, That a Report was to have been spread at the same time of the Queen's Death; no man can tell what might have been the Event." [31] In actuality, Marlborough, upon hearing of the affair, decided not to come into London, remaining at Greenwich until November 19.[32] But the government was anxious to justify its rather peremptory seizure of the images as an action essential to the safety of the nation and the prevention of treason; a Whig demonstration just at the beginning of a crucial parliamentary session could hardly be ignored. The Whigs, for their part, professed the innocence of their plans and hinted that the prevention of such a procession was simply one more indication of the Jacobite leanings of the Oxford ministry: "It appear'd very strange, that a popular Rejoycing, so grateful to this Protestant City . . . should, at this Time, be suppress'd." [33]

Steele was implicated in this "conspiracy" simply by his membership in the Kit-Kat Club, for that society was charged by the Tories with organizing and planning the procession. But in some accounts at the time he was also singled out as having played a leading role in the affair. Peter Wentworth wrote to his brother:

The Whigs . . . are very angry that they were not permited to go on with their supscribtions for burning the Divil and the Pope &c., all their fine figures being seized by a warrant from Lord Dartmouth, and the train bands out to prevent any tumult, for there has been information that the Duke of Montague, Edgecomb, and Steel were to be at the head of the Mob that was to have made this procession; if so I know nobody has more reason to be thankfull 'twas prevented.[34]

Steele was also mentioned in the "Grub Street account" of the affair, which was written by Mrs. Manley at Swift's direction. This pamphlet, *A True Relation of the Several Facts and Circumstances of the Intended Riot and Tumult on Queen Elizabeth's Birth-day,* makes the usual Tory charges. According to this version, Wharton was primarily responsible for the proposed "insurrection," Marlborough was to make an appearance and be greeted by cries of "No Peace," and acts of mob violence were to be encouraged by spreading reports of the Queen's death. Steele, Mrs. Manley asserts, was to have assisted in burning the city:

The Spectator, who ought to be but a looker on, was to have been an assistant, that, seeing London in a flame, he might have opportunity to paint after the life, and remark the behaviour of the people in the ruin of their country, so to have made a diverting Spectator.[35]

Steele must have been annoyed by such absurd accusations, for the *Spectator* on two separate occasions, Nos. 262 and 269, belittled the entire incident; in the latter essay Addison has Sir Roger inquire, " 'Tell me truly, . . . don't you think Sir Andrew had a hand in the Pope's procession?' " [36]

Swift, incidentally, was able several years later to make ironic use of this affair in the course of an attack on Bishop Burnet. In *A Preface to the B—p of S-r-m's Introduction,* he satirizes Burnet's alarmism about the danger of the introduction of Popery into England, remarking that the Bishop must believe himself to be living during the reign of Queen Mary. He continues:

What would he say, to behold the *Fires kindled in* Smithfield, *and all over the Town* on the seventeenth of *November;* to behold the *Pope* born in Triumph on the Shoulders of the People, with a

Cardinal on the one Side, and the Pretender on the other? He
would never believe it was Queen *Elizabeth*'s Days, but that of her
persecuting Sister: In short, how easily might a *Windmill be taken
for* the *Whore of* Babylon, and a *Puppet-Show* for a Popish Procession? [37]

The irony, of course, rests in his adducing as an example in such
a context the procession which the Whigs themselves had
planned.

A second issue affecting the relations between Swift and Steele
in the winter of 1711/12, one more important if less spectacular
than the procession on Elizabeth's "birthday," centered on the
Duke of Marlborough. The Oxford ministry, as we have seen,
considered the discrediting of the Duke essential to the progress
of their peace negotiations, and late in 1711 the campaign against
him intensified, culminating with the formulation of charges
against him for peculation and his dismissal at the end of the
year. Swift's share in this program of turning popular opinion
against the man so idolized by Steele deserves some additional
comment. His indictment of Marlborough in *The Conduct of
the Allies,* published in November, has already been mentioned;
earlier he had become involved in a dispute with the man responsible for the most effective answer to the *Conduct,* Dr.
Francis Hare, Marlborough's Chaplain General. Hare had already irritated the ministry by his *Management of the War,* and
early in September he further antagonized the government by
publishing a sermon which had been preached before Marlborough in celebration of the Duke's victory at Bouchain. This
sermon was largely an exhortation to continue the war and
resist the temptation of making an early peace; as such, of course,
it was extremely offensive to the Tories. St. John wrote William
Harrison, then secretary to the British ambassador at The Hague:

I forgot to tell you, that in a letter to Harry Watkins, you will do
well to observe from what I write to you, that the Examiner is
silent, but that my Lord Marlborough's stupid Chaplain continues
to spoil paper. They had best for their patron's sake, as well as
their own, be quiet. I know how to . . . revive fellows that will
write them to death.[38]

A few weeks later he complained to the Queen about Hare's activities. The "fellows" whom St. John threatened to set upon

Hare evidently included Swift and Mrs. Manley, for early in October appeared *A Learned Comment upon Dr. Hare's Excellent Sermon,* written by Mrs. Manley with the assistance of Swift. This is one of the least successful Tory pamphlets, consisting merely of selected quotations from the sermon followed by heavily ironic remarks. Marlborough receives a few glancing blows, but for the most part the criticism is directed at Hare's insistence on continuing the war.

Somewhat more effective is *A New Vindication of the Duke of Marlborough,* also published early in October and written, Swift tells us, entirely by Mrs. Manley. This was intended as an answer to a pamphlet entitled *Bouchain: Or a Dialogue between the Late Medley and Examiner,* in which the author of the *Examiner* is made to admit his reverence for Marlborough and to apologize for his "Letter to Crassus." [39] Mrs. Manley dismisses this Whig pamphlet very quickly and proceeds to an ironic "defense" of Marlborough which manages, either by insinuation or overt statement, to include almost every charge then being made against the Duke, including that of military ineptitude. Her method here owes a good deal to Swift's *Examiner* No. 16, which had demonstrated ironically that the nation was properly grateful to Marlborough. As Swift had done, Mrs. Manley compares Marlborough's rewards with those of a Roman general and emphasizes his avarice by rhetorical questions, such as, "Is he not the richest and greatest subject in Christendom?" [40] She insinuates, also, that Marlborough's ambition is a dangerous obstacle to the making of a peace and concludes her mock "vindication" with a direct statement concerning the necessity of bringing the war to a close.

Such attacks continued to appear until well after the Duke's dismissal on December 30, although Swift, busy with *The Conduct of the Allies,* contributed little to the campaign except for an incidental line in his bitter indictment of the Duchess of Somerset, *A Windsor Prophecy.* Even though he disliked Marlborough and willingly contributed to a program designed to destroy his popularity, Swift viewed his dismissal with considerable misgivings. Such a rash action, he feared, would have unfortunate effects abroad, and upon hearing that the Duke wished "to contrive some way how to soften Dr. Swift," he protested that he

had not been responsible for those satires which were most
severe.[41]

If Swift was apprehensive about the dismissal of this victorious
general, the Whigs were furious. On January 1, the day after his
loss of command, appeared *The Englishman's Thanks to the
Duke of Marlborough,* written by Richard Steele but signed
"Scoto-Britannus." In this short pamphlet Steele is incredibly
rhetorical in his eulogy of the Duke:

> Accept, O Familiar, O Amiable, O Glorious Man, the Thanks of
> every Generous, every Honest Man in *Great Britain.* . . . While
> You are what You cannot cease to be, that Mild Virtue is Your
> Armour; the Shameless Ruffian that should Attempt to Sully it,
> would find his Force against it as Detestable, as the Strength of a
> Ravisher in the Violation of Chastity; the Testimonies of a Per-
> jur'd Man Confronting Truth, or Clamour drowning the Voice of
> Innocence.[42]

Behind Steele's rhetoric, of course, is a sincere indignation at
the treatment afforded a national hero, but such a style could
hardly escape the ridicule of the Tories. The *Examiner,* which
had been revived on December 6, scornfully pointed out the
stylistic absurdities, but ascribed Steele's pamphlet, either seriously or invidiously, to "an old, sowr, dry Critick, and blasted
Poet," meaning John Dennis.[43] Dennis, in turn, denied authorship of the piece and took occasion to praise Marlborough as
"the greatest Man upon Earth" and to attack Swift as the author
of the *Examiner.* It is interesting to note that Dennis, believing
Swift to be the author of the ridicule of Steele's pamphlet, accuses
him of "selling and betraying" his old friends.[44] Of course he
may be referring simply to Swift's change of parties, since it is
possible that Dennis did not know of Steele's authorship of *The
Englishman's Thanks to the Duke of Marlborough.*

To justify its action in the face of impassioned criticism such
as Steele's, the ministry felt it necessary to continue its journalistic campaign against Marlborough even after his dismissal.
The *Examiner,* in particular, was used for this purpose; every
issue for over a month after his dismissal was devoted almost
exclusively to vitriolic criticism of the Duke, based usually on
the "crimes" with which he had been charged. In the paper of

February 14, for example, the Tory paper, now written by William Oldisworth, both praises Swift's *Conduct of the Allies* and viciously hits at Marlborough. Swift, however, had no desire to be connected with such attacks. He had attempted to lessen the severity of these *Examiners* but had not succeeded; "I'm sure now he is down," he wrote of Marlborough, "I shall not trample on him"—a resolution which he apparently forgot when he composed *A Satirical Elegy* on the Duke's death eleven years later.[45]

As a matter of fact, he continued to contribute to the avalanche of attacks in the early months of 1711/12. Only a few days after the general had been relieved of his command, there appeared a poem entitled *A Fable of the Widow and her Cat,* which at least in part was the work of Swift.[46] Here Marlborough is satirized as the favorite cat who has treacherously stolen his Mistress's cream and who is turned over to the watchdog (Parliament) for punishment. It was answered by the Whigs with *When the Cat's away, the Mice may Play,* inscribed to Swift. This exchange was fairly light in tone. A much more biting satire was Swift's *A Fable of Midas,* published on February 14. These satiric verses first relate the legend of Midas and then make the application to Marlborough:

> This Tale inclines the gentle Reader,
> To think upon a certain *Leader,*
> To whom from *Midas* down, descends
> That Virtue in the Fingers ends:
> What else by *Perquisites* are meant,
> By *Pensions, Bribes,* and *three per Cent?*
> By *Places* and *Commissions* sold
> And turning *Dung* it self to *Gold?*
> By starving in the midst of Store,
> As t'other *Midas* did before? [47]

The allusions are to the charges of embezzlement which had been brought against Marlborough. Swift ends his poem with a description of the modern Midas losing his power by action of the Senate: "And *Midas* now neglected stands, / With *Asses Ears,* and *dirty Hands.*"

In addition to these poems, Swift must be credited with overseeing some prose pamphlets which formed a part of the flood of anti-Marlborough propaganda in January and February. *The Representation of the Loyal Subjects of Albania,* by William Wagstaffe, appeared on January 4. It is a general indictment of the Whigs, especially as prolongers of the war, and the only personal satire which it contains is directed at Marlborough. In the *Journal* for that date Swift speaks of supervising "a pamphlet made by one of my understrappers," which in all probability refers to this piece by Wagstaffe. A second pamphlet by Wagstaffe was published in February, entitled *The Story of St. Alb—ns Ghost, Or the Apparition of Mother Haggy.* It is devoted entirely to an attack on the Marlboroughs, "Mother Haggy" representing the mother of the Duchess. She is depicted as a notorious witch, whose daughter Haggite marries Avaro (the Duke of Marlborough). His activities together with those of the Whig Junto are then satirized, the allegory concluding with the appearance of Mother Haggy's ghost at a meeting of the Junto and Marlborough plotting against the Queen. The entire group is doomed, the apparition informs them; the Duke and Duchess of Marlborough will fall, a sacrifice to their own ambition and avarice. Swift's comment on his connection with this satire is characteristically ambiguous: "Lady Masham made me read to her a pretty 2 penny Pamphlet calld the St Albans Ghost. I thought I had writt it my self; so did they, but I did not." [48] Since there is no more evidence than this for assigning a share in the pamphlet to Swift, it must be considered in its entirety as the work of his "understrapper" Wagstaffe, in whose *Miscellaneous Works* it was later reprinted.[49]

With these poems and pamphlets written or directed by Swift to justify Marlborough's dismissal to the popular mind must be contrasted Steele's veneration for the general.[50] In November of this year, as the Duke was preparing to go into voluntary exile, Steele dedicated to him the fourth volume of the collected *Spectator.* There he took occasion once more to defend the subject of his eulogy from Tory attacks. It should be noted that in the opinion of Miss Blanchard, "the Duke of Marlborough was the rock upon which the friendship of Steele and Swift split." She finds the "seat of the trouble" to be "Steele's smouldering resentment of Swift's share in the flood of propaganda from 1710 on against Marlborough, for whom his admiration was not only political but personal." [51] Her point, I think, is somewhat over-stated. After Swift's alignment with the Harley ministry, a con-tinuation of his friendship with Steele, whom he had never re-spected as he did Addison, became simply impossible. Both their estrangement of these years and its eruption into open antag-onism in 1713 were the result of a complex of issues, involving differences of conviction, differences of temperament, and the gradual accumulation of a series of incidents which made man-ifest their conflicting interests and loyalties. The question of the Duke of Marlborough was certainly one of the most important sources of bad feeling, but it seems to me unnecessary to single out one issue as dominant in anything as nebulous and unpre-dictable as human relationships.

3.

During 1712, Swift, Steele, and Addison continued along separate political paths. Addison this year was acting as an intermediary between the Hanoverian representative in England and the Whig leaders. He assisted in the drafting of Hanoverian official papers and was involved in secret negotiations designed to safe-guard the Succession against possible Jacobite plots.[52] The *Spec-tator* continued its subtle disparagement of the landed interest; and other Whig motifs appeared as the occasion arose. The four volumes of the collected *Spectator* published in the course of the year were all dedicated to Whig potentates: Somers, Halifax, Boyle, and Marlborough.

Swift, meanwhile, was writing steadily in support of the gov-ernment. *Some Remarks on the Barrier Treaty,* designed to sup-plement *The Conduct of the Allies,* appeared in February. Two other pamphlets in the early months of the year were more conciliatory and aimed at winning the extremists of both parties to the support of Oxford's moderate ministry. These were *A Letter to the October Club,* an appeal to the extreme element among the Tories to remain loyal to the Lord Treasurer despite their impatience at what seemed to them his half measures, and *Some Reasons to prove That no Person is obliged by his Prin-ciples, as a Whig, to oppose Her Majesty, or her Present Ministry. In a letter to a Whig Lord.* The latter tract is particularly inter-esting, for, as Davis points out, the arguments which it presents may be taken as a sincere expression of the moderate point of view which underlay Swift's alliance with the Harley–St. John group.[53] His entire point is that principles are not in question, that the policies pursued by the government are such that any "Whig" can support. Once again he impugns the validity of party terminology, asserting that differences between the present "Whigs" and "Tories" arise not from principles but from personal allegiances:

> I can truly affirm, That none of the reasonable sober *Whigs* I have conversed with, did ever avow any Opinion concerning Religion or Government, which I was not willing to subscribe; so that, according to my Judgment, those Terms of Distinction ought to be dropped, and others introduced in their stead, to denominate Men, as they are inclined to *Peace* or *War*, to the *Last*, or the *Present Ministry:* For whoever thoroughly considers the matter, will find these to be the only Differences that divide the Nation at present.[54]

Surely there is no Whig, he goes on to say, that will openly deny the Queen's prerogative to change her ministry or make a peace.

Although in 1712 circumstances did not yet compel Swift and Steele to write against each other, personal attacks upon Swift by the friends of Addison and Steele were common enough. Thomas Burnet lashed out at Swift in *Our Ancestors as wise as we,* written in January in defense of Marlborough. Steele apparently had some connection with this work, for Burnet wrote to his friend George Duckett, "I am entirely satisfyd in your opinion of my Book, Steel objected to the very same passages in it."[55] Duckett answered Swift's *Windsor Prophecy* with "A Prophecy of Merlin's, as it was found in M—r's Hole," printed in the *Protestant Post Boy* for May 20. And Burnet later in the year again hit at Swift in *A Certain Information of a Certain Discourse,* where Swift, Atterbury, Prior, and Defoe are attacked as "mercenary Pen-sellers" and the ministers are reminded that if they give preferment to the author of *A Tale of a Tub* they will show themselves as "Supporters of Atheism and Prophaneness."[56] Of course, the situation was sometimes reversed, with Steele the object of occasional satiric thrusts by Swift's friends. Thus in Arbuthnot's *The Art of Political Lying,* which had been read in manuscript by Swift, reference is made to a "hot-headed, crack-brained coxcomb," which is perhaps meant to suggest Steele, since it appears in a context of personal allusions.

In May of 1712 Swift was attacked once more by friends of Steele, this time for his publication of *A Proposal for Correcting, Improving and Ascertaining the English Tongue*, in the form of a letter to Oxford and bearing Swift's signature. Professor Louis Landa has pointed out the extent to which this *Proposal*, with its extended eulogy of Harley, is a party document designed partially to alienate the Whigs so that credit for the formation of an Academy could rest solely with the Tories.[57] Deserving Whigs were to be included, however, in this project for "fixing our language forever," for Swift wrote to Archbishop King that he and Harley had named as members twenty men of both parties. He had first considered the subject of the present tract in Steele's *Tatler* (No. 230); Addison had devoted a *Spectator* essay (No. 135) to the question, paying tribute to Swift at the same time; and it may be assumed that Swift expected at least one of these estranged friends to participate in his current program. Such, at any rate, is indicated by a passage complimenting Steele in this *Proposal:*

> Besides, I would willingly avoid Repetition; having about a Year ago, communicated to the Publick, much of what I had to offer upon this Subject, by the Hands of an ingenious Gentleman, who for a long Time did thrice a Week divert or instruct the Kingdom by his Papers; and is supposed to pursue the same Design at present, under the Title of *Spectator*. [In a Conversation some Time ago with the Person to whom these Productions are ascribed, I happened to mention the Proposall I have here made to Your Lordship; and in a few dayes after I observed that Author had taken the Hint and treated the same matter in one of his Papers, and with much Judgement, except where he is pleased to put so great a Compliment upon me, as I can never pretend to Deserve.] This Author, who hath tried the Force and Compass of our Language with so much Success, agrees entirely with me in most of my Sentiments relating to it.[58]

A year later, when the dispute between the two men was at its height, Swift took occasion to remind Steele of this compliment:

> You cannot but remember, that in the only thing I ever published with my name, I took care to celebrate you as much as I could, and in as handsome a manner, though it was in a letter to the present Lord Treasurer.[59]

Despite this conciliatory gesture toward Steele, his friends could hardly afford to let Swift's tract pass unnoticed. John Oldmixon's *Reflections on Dr. Swift's Letter to the Earl of Oxford* makes the usual charges against Swift of political apostasy and irreligion, at the same time ridiculing his plan for stabilizing the language. A second pamphlet, *The British Academy,* forgoes such personal abuse of Swift in favor of a less direct but more effective attack on the scheme by an ironic comparison of the Tory proposals with the procedures of the French Academy. Chiefly responsible for this rejoinder was Arthur Maynwaring, a close associate of Steele's; the identity of his collaborators is not known, but they may have included any of the better-known Whig writers, such as Burnet, Duckett, Henley, or possibly even Steele himself.[60]

In this same month, May, 1712, Steele and Swift were brought into direct conflict when the *Spectator* reprinted a Preface to Four Sermons by William Fleetwood, Bishop of St. Asaph.[61] Steele begins the issue (No. 384 for May 21) with an excerpt from the Tory *Post Boy* which censures Baron Bothmar, the Hanoverian envoy to England, and refers to "Republican" efforts to spread reports of the Pretender's death. This "Jacobite" paragraph, so placed as to contrast with the ideas of the Bishop's Preface, is followed by a few introductory remarks and then the text of Fleetwood's Preface. Although on the surface the Preface is merely the Bishop's explanation of why he chose to publish these sermons, it manages to convey nearly all the major Whig propaganda themes: the danger to the Protestant Succession, the association of "Popery and arbitrary power" with the Tory administration, praise of the Duke of Marlborough, disparagement of the Tory peace, and eulogy of the seven years of "Whig" government. A few weeks after the *Spectator* carried the Preface, it was condemned by the House of Commons and burned by the common Hangman.

Steele's purpose in using an entire issue of the *Spectator* for a reprint of the Preface was to give this significant Opposition polemic a much wider audience than it would normally have had. The Bishop himself testified that the device was successful; in a letter to the Bishop of Salisbury, he remarked, "The SPECTATOR has conveyed above 14,000 of them into other People's

Hands, that would otherwise have never seen or heard of it." [62] As a result, the Tory writers who attacked the Preface, including Swift, were careful to include Steele in their condemnation of Fleetwood and his pamphlet.

Swift's first contribution to the Fleetwood controversy was called *A Letter of Thanks from my Lord Wharton to the Lord Bᵖ of S. Asaph, In the Name of the Kit-Cat-Club.* By writing ironically in the guise of Wharton, Swift is able to level his attack simultaneously against the Whigs in general, Fleetwood and his Preface, Steele and the Kit-Kat Club, and Wharton himself. In the first paragraph Steele is indicted as the primary means by which the Bishop's views were disseminated:

> It was with no little Satisfaction I undertook the pleasing Task, assigned me by the Gentlemen of the *Kit-Cat-Club,* of addressing your Lordship with Thanks for your late Service so seasonally done to our Sinking Cause, in reprinting those most excellent Discourses, which you had formerly preached with so great Applause, though they were never heard of by us, till they were recommended to our Perusal by the *Spectator,* who some time since, in one of his Papers, entertained the Town with a Paragraph out of the *Post-Boy,* and your Lordship's extraordinary *Preface.*[63]

Swift makes no real attempt to answer Fleetwood's arguments, contenting himself largely with ridicule of his style. His device for satirizing the style of the Preface is an extended mock encomium, in the course of which the *Spectator* is again mentioned:

> Who can read, unmov'd, these following Strokes of Oratory? *Such was the Fame, Such was the Reputation, Such was the Faithfulness and Zeal, to Such a Height of Military Glory,* . . . &c. O! the irresistible Charm of the Word *Such!* Well, since *Erasmus* wrote a Treatise in Praise of Folly; and my Lord *Rochester* an excellent Poem upon *Nothing,* I am resolved to employ the *Spectator,* or some of his Fraternity, (Dealers in Words) to write an Encomium upon SUCH.[64]

Equally devastating though less bantering in tone was Swift's second attack on Fleetwood, in the *Examiner* for July 24. Here Swift seeks to embarrass the Bishop by retrieving a separate preface to one of his sermons which had not been included in the new edition. In that preface, written in 1700, Fleetwood seemed to attack the Whigs as *"an impudent and clamorous Faction,"* and Swift is thus afforded an excellent opportunity for sarcasm at this evidence of a change in politics. As justification for reprinting this earlier preface in its entirety, Swift cites the precedent of Steele, who, he suggests, was well paid by the Whigs for his service to them in *Spectator* No. 384:

> I have chose to set it at length, to prevent which might be objected against me, as an unfair Representer; should I reserve any part of this admirable Discourse, as well as to imitate the judicious *Spectator,* tho' I fear I shall not have such goodly Contributions from our Party as that Author is said to have from another upon the like Occasion; or if I chance to give offence, be promised to have my Losses made up to me, for my great Zeal in circulating *Prefaces. . . .*[65]

The usual parade of Grub Street pamphlets made its appearance in this controversy, and in many of them Steele was either criticized or defended. Those which attacked Fleetwood and Steele, such as *The Speech of John Ketch, Esq; at the Burning of a late scandalous and malitious Preface,* were sometimes attributed to Swift in the Whig press.[66] More important than these pamphlets, however, was the campaign against Steele in the *Plain Dealer,* a Tory periodical which ran for seventeen numbers between April 12 and August 2, 1712. This paper was apparently the work of William Wagstaffe, for it is reprinted in his *Miscellaneous Works* (1726). Wagstaffe, a somewhat shadowy figure whose anti-Marlborough pamphlets have already been mentioned, played a fairly important role in the relations between Swift and Steele. Besides the *Plain Dealer,* his *Works* included a number of other Tory pamphlets dating from the Queen Anne period, of which the most significant was *The Character of Richard Steele,* an abusive personal attack which first appeared in 1713. Steele, as we shall see, believed this work to have been written by Swift, and indeed both in his own day and in the nineteenth century Swift was thought to have written a number of the pieces included in Wagstaffe's volume. Certainly, Steele or any of his friends reading the *Plain Dealer's* assault on the *Spectator* for its dissemination of Fleetwood's Preface would have been tempted to see Swift's hand at work. For one thing, the Tory paper begins its attack by singling out the "Observations of the *Indian Kings*" and the essays on the "Humours of Sir *Roger*" as valuable contributions of the sort to which the *Spectator* should confine itself; the former, of course, was based completely on a suggestion by Swift which he regretted having given to Steele. Then, after ridiculing the *Spectator*'s claim to impartiality in politics and accusing Steele of propagating "ill principles," Wagstaffe closes with a curious paragraph directed at Steele, one which in tone could perhaps have been mistaken for Swift's:

> Whatsoever I have said is in order to correct some Mistakes, upon due Reflexion, you may find your self guilty of; and I hope you cannot suppose that because you are capable of reforming others, you are altogether perfect in your self. My Person is concealed, and shall continue so, though I should gain as great a Reputation by my Works, as you have done by Yours, which I have not the Vanity to expect: And if what I have done out of no other Consideration but your Good, without any Design of entering into a Paper-Quarrel, should occasion one, I must act so far the *Plain Dealer* as to tell you, tho' I am willing to be your Friend, yet . . . I am not afraid to be your Adversary.[67]

Nor did the *Plain Dealer* end its attack on Steele with that issue. The numbers for June 28 and July 12, 1712, relate the adventures of "Dick Hotspur," who is clearly a figure for the Whigs in general and Richard Steele in particular.[68] Steele's notorious love of "projects," for example, is satirized. On the back of one of Dick Hotspur's papers are found some jottings headed "the Raree-show Project":

> "Several Persons of Distinction, to make their Cavalcade through the City, Mum. —White Horse at *Aldgate* — Mother Dead, —*Leaden-Hall Street*, —All Right — Beer and Brandy in Abundance, — Glorious — Long live *Fortunatus*, —*Bouchain, cum multis aliis* — Huzza —Hey for St. *James's*, Boys, —*York-Buildings* in Jeopardy, —Part two-a-Clock, —*Lord Protector*, —*General* for Life, —Same Thing in Greek — the Day's our own — Hah, hah, hah. —"[69]

This, I think, is almost certainly intended as ridicule of the Whig procession planned for Queen Elizabeth's "birthday," the

"Raree-show" alluding to the images to be used in the procession, "General for life" to the role the Tories alleged Marlborough was to play in the affair, and "Mother Dead" to the rumors of the Queen's death which the Whigs were supposed to spread. It is interesting that, seven months after the event, a government writer still thought it would be effective to remind the public of Steele's share in the "plot" of November 17.

In view of their contrasting activities in connection with such party issues as the publication of Fleetwood's Preface, it is hardly surprising that Swift, Steele, and Addison had little occasion for friendly meetings in the second half of 1712, although Swift does record an exchange of visits with Addison in July. A few days after this meeting, Swift again attacked Addison's patron the Earl of Wharton in *A Letter from the Pretender, to a Whig-Lord,* a rather heavy-handed effort to turn back against the Whigs their accusations of Tory Jacobitism. Steele he seldom mentioned and never saw. He did, however, take note in the *Journal* of Steele's unfortunate blunder in proposing a lottery, called the Multiplication Table, on the very day that Parliament passed an act against illegal lotteries. After reporting to Stella that Steele was under prosecution, an assertion which apparently was incorrect, Swift again reveals his attitude about the recent political activity of the *Spectator:* "I believe he will very soon lose his Employmt, for he has been mighty impertinent of late in his Spectators, and I will never offer a Word in his behalf." [70] Steele's publication of *Spectator* No. 384 had brought him in danger of losing his post in the Stamp Commission. A letter from Steele to Oxford in August, in which he refers to the minister's "generous treatment," leads Miss Blanchard to believe that Steele once again kept his office only through the intercession of the Lord Treasurer.[71]

The *Spectator* and periodicals more overtly political in nature felt the effect of St. John's Stamp Act, which took force in July and dampened the ardor of many party journalists. By this Act, all periodicals of a half sheet or less were taxed a halfpenny and those of a whole sheet one penny. For the *Observator,* the *Medley,* and the *Plain Dealer,* this meant the end; the *Examiner,* though "deadly sick," in Swift's phrase, continued to print, and the *Spectator* doubled its price. The purpose of the Act, from the government point of view, was to diminish the output of the

Opposition press, but its efficacy in this respect was limited. Whig propaganda continued unabated.[72]

In the closing months of 1712 there was ample material for party journalists. Feeling was stirred by the famous duel on November 15 between the Tory Duke of Hamilton and the Whig Lord Mohun. The Duke, newly appointed as ambassador to France, died from wounds which the Tories, including Swift, maintained Mohun's second, General Maccartney, had inflicted after the duel itself was over. The Whigs insisted that Hamilton's death had been a regrettable accident, whereas the Tory version, represented by Swift's "malicious" account in the *Post Boy*, saw his death as the result of a Whig plot.[73] Shortly before this duel, Swift had been involved in another "plot," similarly exploited by the press of both sides. A bandbox which concealed a pistol and a firing device had been sent to Oxford and discovered by Swift, who disarmed the mechanism. The Tories, of course, tried to make political capital of the incident by describing it as an attempted assassination planned by the Whigs, who in turn accused Swift of having manufactured the entire affair. For example, George Duckett, the minor Whig writer who was a friend of Burnet's and an acquaintance of Steele's, satirized Swift's role in the "plot" in a piece entitled "A Great Plot! The Second Part of St. Paul's Screw-Plot! Or, Mine A—se in a Ban-Box," published in the *Flying Post* for November 22.[74]

On December 6, 1712, the *Spectator* ceased publication, partly because of the effect of the Stamp Act and partly because its authors now wished to turn their energies in other directions. Addison was finally contemplating a production of his *Cato,* and Steele had already determined to initiate a new periodical in which he could comment more directly on political affairs. During the following year his political writing in this new journal, the *Guardian,* was to make him one of the leading Whig propagandists and the direct antagonist of Swift. On December 26, 1712, Swift reported an accidental meeting with Addison and Philips which prompted him to a general reflection on his estrangement from these former companions:

> I mett Mr Addison and pastorall Philips on the Mall to day, & took a Turn with them; But they both looked terrible dry and cold; a Curse of Party; and do you know that I have taken more pains

to recommend the Whig Witts to the Favor & mercy of the Ministers than any other People. Steel I have kept in his Place; Congreve I have got to be used kindly and secured. Row I have recommended, and got a Promise of a Place; Philips I shoud certainly
have provided for if he had not run Party-mad and made me with-
draw my Recommendation; and I sett Addison so right at first
that he might have been employd; and have partly secured him
the Place he has. Yet I am worse used by that Faction than any
man.[75]

The difficulties in their relationship are put by Swift in purely
personal terms, of resentment arising from favors offered and
from offers refused or ungratefully accepted. But of course the
matter went deeper than that. The "Curse of Party" which had
thus split the leading writers of Queen Anne's England involved
conflicting loyalties and convictions which became more apparent
with each new political incident or public issue. As the question
of the Tory Peace gave way in 1713 and 1714 to the more emotional issue of the Protestant Succession, the hostility between
Swift and the Whig wits could only become intensified.

4

THE PEACE,
THE SUCCESSION,
AND AFTER

THE LAST two years of the reign of Anne were marked by an extreme tension in domestic politics, a tension which communicated itself to the opposing ranks of Whig and Tory writers. Though the Peace of Utrecht afforded a temporary relaxation, a new outbreak of political hostilities quickly ensued over the touchy issue of the Protestant Succession, which brought party warfare to its greatest intensity since the beginning of the Oxford ministry. For those like Swift who belonged to the inner circles of the government, anxiety over this political situation was aggravated by the internal conflict among the Tories themselves; the struggle for power between Oxford and Bolingbroke seemed certain to bring disaster. It was almost inevitable at such a time that literary rivalry and political sympathies should become more closely connected than ever, with Addison and Swift both attempting to win over to their groups an important neutral like Pope. In the area of political writing, the atmosphere of uncertainty, fear, and personal animosity which surrounded issues like Dunkirk and the Succession was reflected by a flood of virulent and abusive pamphlets. Steele and Swift, now bitter enemies, assumed the roles of leading propagandists in this violent eruption of party warfare.

1.

There was, however, a calm before this storm. In the early spring of 1713, when the successful conclusion of the peace negotiations had become assured, literary Whigs and Tories engaged in a general movement toward reconciliation. Swift began meeting once more with Addison and Steele; and Addison's *Cato* provided a common ground for the re-establishment of amicable relations. Of course political pamphleteering did not altogether cease. Swift, in January, published *Mr. Collins's Discourse of Free-Thinking, Put into Plain English, by Way of Abstract, for the Use of the Poor,* an ironic attack on Collins which seeks in the usual way to connect "free-thinking" with the Whig party; and, in March, Steele also produced a pamphlet, entitled *A Letter to Sir M. W. Concerning Occasional Peers.* Provoked by rumors that the Queen was about to repeat her successful experiment of ensuring a Tory majority in Lords by creating new peers, he depicts the practice as dangerous to the Constitution and proposes a bill to prohibit any peer from voting until three years after the date of his patent. For the most part, though, these months were characterized by a general easing of tension between Swift and the Whig wits.

In February he and his former friends met at the funeral of Swift's Whig protégé, William Harrison: "His brothere Poets bury'd him, as Mr. Addison, Mr. Philips, and Dr. Swift." [1] But there was no opportunity here for friendly overtures; Swift, much affected by the death of Harrison, did not even mention the presence of Addison in his account of the funeral to Stella. Nor were the Whig writers in any mood for conciliatory gestures. George Berkeley, then in London, was well received by both Swift and Steele, despite his Tory sympathies; on February 23, he reported that Addison and Steele were "entirely persuaded" that the ministers were engaged in a Jacobite plot.[2] Nevertheless, a month later Steele was attempting to enlist the support of Ox-

ford for his private theater "the Censorium," a project which, like
Swift's Academy, was to include both Whigs and Tories. That he
was now on good terms with Harley is further indicated by an
undated letter concerning the project which probably belongs
to these months.[3] On March 27, Berkeley corrected his earlier
report that Steele suspected the ministry of Jacobite intrigues.
At the same time, he described a breakfast with Addison and
Swift which seemed to him to promise an early cessation of party
hostilities:

> Mr Steele having told me this week that he now imagines my
> Lord Treasurer had no design of bringing in the Pretender, and in
> case he had, that he is persuaded he could never perform it; and
> this morning I breakfasted with Mr Addison at Dr Swift's lodging.
> His coming in whilst I was there, and the good temper he shewed,
> was construed by me as a sign of an approaching coalition of par-
> ties, Mr Addison being more earnest in the Whig cause than Mr
> Steele (the former having quitted an employment, rather than
> hold it under the Tories, which by a little compliance he might
> have done), and there having passed a coldness, if not a direct
> breach, between those two gentlemen and Dr Swift on the score of
> politics.[4]

On the following day Addison attended a "mighty Levee" held
by Swift. Berkeley's prediction that these meetings signified a
political "coalition" was supported by the fact that Oxford at
this time was holding a series of talks with Whig leaders. These
negotiations came to little as far as the structure of the parties
was concerned, but they at least encouraged a parallel movement
toward settling political differences in the literary world.

Swift was willing to do his share in making relations more
cordial. On the first of April he announced to Stella that he had
arranged a meeting between Addison and Bolingbroke:

> I prevaild on Ld Bol— to invite Mr Addison to dine with him
> on good Friday; I suppose we shall be mighty mannerly. Addison
> is to have a play of his acted on Friday in Easter week; tis a
> Tragedy called Cato. I saw it unfinished some Years ago: did I tell
> you, tht Steel has begun a new daily Paper calld the Guardian,
> they say good for nothing; I have not seen it.[5]

Steele's *Guardian*, which Swift here disparages, had begun on
March 12. It is a further index to the spirit of these weeks that

for over a month Steele's paper contained nothing political and
that among its contributors were such Tories as Berkeley and
Parnell. Addison's dinner with Bolingbroke occurred as planned
on April 3, just after the signing of the Peace of Utrecht. Swift's
account shows it to have been a successful affair, where political
differences were aired without heat:

> Addison & I & some others dined with Ld Bol— and sate with him
> till 12; we were very Civil, but yet when we grew warm, we talkt
> in a friendly manner of Party, Addison raised his Objections, & Ld
> Bol— answered them with great Complaisance. Addison began Ld
> Sommers Health, wch went about; but I bid him not name Ld
> Wh—'s for I would not pledge it, and I tod Ld Bol— frankly that
> Addison loved Ld Wh— as little as I did. so we laughed &c—[6]

It may have been somewhat unrealistic of Swift to report so
confidently Addison's dislike of Wharton; however much Addison may have disapproved of his immorality, he respected the
Earl's political principles and his tactical shrewdness. Only a
week after Swift made this remark, the fifth volume of the *Spectator* appeared, with a laudatory dedication to Wharton.

Meanwhile, preparations were under way for the production
of Addison's *Cato*. On April 6, Swift attended a rehearsal and
later dined privately with Addison. Eight days later the play
had its first performance and was prodigiously successful. The
way in which both parties, in a friendly manner, interpreted
the play as embodying either Whig or Tory principles is a familiar story. The *Guardian* praised the play without making
any political application; and the *Examiner,* in accord with
government policy, gave a favorable review, although it condemned Steele for allegedly prompting a Whig claque in the
theater. Perhaps the most amusing comment on the Tory interpretation of Cato as a minister opposed to a "perpetual dictator"
(i.e., Marlborough) was made by Thomas Burnet: "But I go yet
farther and will allow either St Johns or H. to be Catos, when
they'll please to stab themselves, as he did." [7]

On April 23, in the midst of Addison's literary triumph, the
warrants were signed to make Swift Dean of St. Patrick's. He
began making preparations for departure to Ireland, but before
he actually left England, on June 1, he saw the end of the cordial

relations which he had re-established with the Whig wits. The friendly atmosphere had lasted only a short two months. On April 28, Steele printed a letter in *Guardian* No. 41 which attacked the *Examiner* in the harshest terms for its reflection upon the Earl of Nottingham and his daughter. This was promptly answered by the *Examiner* of May 8, which also used the fictitious "letter" device to reply to Steele. Much of the Tory rejoinder is merely *tu quoque*, reminding Steele of his own political satires in the *Tatler,* such as the letter from Downes the prompter. The *Examiner* is urged not to answer the "Scurrility" of the *Guardian,* but to " 'let it lie as you find it in the Corner of his Paper, close by the Royal Stamp' "—a hint to Steele of his obligations to the Queen and the government because of his post in the Stamp Office.[8]

Shortly after this exchange, Steele wrote a related *Guardian* which immediately provoked an open break with Swift. No. 53 (May 12) consists of a letter to "Nestor Ironside" signed with Steele's own name. In it he answers the *Examiner*'s accusations against the *Tatler* by disclaiming responsibility for some of its political satires and denying the satiric intention of others. He then reviews the *Examiner*'s aspersions on Nottingham's daughter, which had prompted his earlier "letter," and calls upon the *Guardian* to defend Marlborough and the Junto from the slanderous attacks of the Tory paper. About the authorship of the *Examiner* he has this to say:

> "However, I will not bear hard upon his contrition; but am now heartily sorry I called him a miscreant, that word I think signifies an unbeliever. *Mescroyant,* I take it, is the old French word. I will give myself no manner of liberty to make guesses at him, if I may say him: for though sometimes I have been told by familiar friends, that they saw me such a time talking to the Examiner; others, who have rallied me upon the sins of my youth, tell me it is credibly reported that I have formerly lain with the Examiner. I have carried my point, and rescued innocence from calumny; and it is nothing to me, whether the Examiner writes against me in the character of an estranged friend or an exasperated mistress." [9]

The allusions, of course, are to Mrs. Manley and Swift; his byplay with the term "miscreant" is intended as a reflection upon Swift's position as a clergyman.

As a result of *Guardian* No. 53, angry recriminations between Swift and Steele began at once. On the following day, Swift wrote in rather formal terms to Addison, protesting that Steele had reflected upon him in his paper, a fact, he says, he could hardly believe until he sent for the *Guardian* himself. He continues:

> I found he had, in several parts of it, insinuated with the utmost malice, that I was author of the Examiner; and abused me in the grossest manner he could possibly invent, and sent his name to what he had written. Now, Sir, if I am not author of the Examiner, how will Mr. Steele be able to defend himself from the imputation of the highest degree of baseness, ingratitude, and injustice? Is he so ignorant of my temper, and of my style? Has he never heard that the author of the Examiner, to whom I am altogether a stranger, did a month or two ago vindicate me from having any concern in it? Should not Mr. Steele have first expostulated with me as a friend? Have I deserved this usage from Mr. Steele, who knows very well that my Lord Treasurer has kept him in his employment upon my entreaty and intercession?

Addison, however, was not inclined to seek a peaceful solution to the quarrel. He merely turned Swift's series of questions over to Steele, who, on May 19, wrote a reply. He begins:

> Mr. Addison showed me your letter, wherein you mention me. They laugh at you, if they make you believe your interposition has kept me thus long in my office. If you have spoken in my behalf at any time, I am glad I have always treated you with respect; though I believe you an accomplice of the Examiner's.[10]

Steele then points out that Swift has not directly denied a connection with the *Examiner* but has merely cited as proof that paper's declaration of his innocence. He ends his letter with congratulations on Swift's preferment.

Steele's phrase "they laugh at you" stung Swift's pride; he refers to it five times in the course of the angry rejoinder he sent Steele on May 23, and it is clear that he was totally ignorant of the friendly relations Steele had been secretly maintaining with Harley.[11] In his answer Swift describes the extent to which he has solicited on Steele's behalf. He continues:

This is the history of what you think fit to call, in the spirit of insulting, their laughing at me; and you may do it securely, for, by
the most inhuman dealings, you have wholly put it out of my
power, as a Christian, to do you the least ill office. . . . And, once
more, suppose they did laugh at me, I ask whether my inclinations
to serve you merit to be rewarded by the vilest treatment, whether
they succeeded or not? If your interpretation were true, I was
laughed at only for your sake; which, I think, is going pretty far
to serve a friend.[12]

He again disclaims any connection with the writing of the present
Examiner and asserts that when he had been involved in such
matters a few years ago he had consistently struck out any reflections upon Addison or Steele in manuscripts submitted for
his approval. Finally, he enters a general protest against Steele's
attack upon him: "There are solecisms in morals as well as in
languages; and to which of the virtues you will reconcile your
conduct to me, is past my imagination."

Meanwhile, the *Examiner,* in its issue of May 22, had brought
this personal quarrel into the Tory press:

I sometime ago acquitted a *Certain Gentleman* of having any share
in this *Paper;* Yet I observe in three or four Passages of Mr. *Steele's*
Letter, there are some malicious Glances at *That Gentleman,*
which as he never deserv'd from the World, so, if my Information
fail me not, he has deserv'd them least of all the World from Mr.
Steele, both as an *Author,* and as One YET in Employment.[13]

Oldisworth then decries Steele's slanderous remarks about Mrs.
Manley.

Before Steele replied either to Swift's letter or this *Examiner,*
he wrote a rough draft of a letter of resignation from his remaining government post, that of Commissioner of the Stamp Office.
He gives as the reason for his resignation his intention to stand
for Parliament. In the draft, as contrasted with the version
actually sent to Oxford on June 4, Steele details his reasons for
attacking the *Examiner* in his *Guardian* and tactfully reproaches
Oxford for allowing a government writer to traduce Marlborough
and the Junto.[14] Then, as an answer to the *Examiner's* attack
on his references to an "estranged friend" and an "exasperated
mistress," he wrote another *Guardian* which must have been

as offensive to Swift as the paper which had provoked their present altercation. "There has been named for this paper one, for whom I have a value," he writes, meaning Swift, and he continues in much the same vein as his private letters to Swift:

> I have named no man, but if there be any gentleman, who wrongfully lies under the imputation of being, or assisting the Examiner, he would do well to do himself justice, under his own hand, in the eye of the world.[15]

As for Mrs. Manley, Steele writes, "I can now make her no reparation, but in begging her pardon, that I never lay with her." After this sally, Steele censures the *Examiner* for its flattery and "nauseous applause" of Oxford and Bolingbroke.

A few days later, on May 26, Steele sent his last letter to Swift, an extraordinarily self-righteous document in which hostility toward Swift gives way to a statement of his own integrity. He writes:

> I am obliged to you for any kind things said in my behalf to the Treasurer; and assure you, when you were in Ireland, you were the constant subject of my talk to men in power at that time. As to the vilest of mankind, it would be a glorious world if I were: for I would not conceal my thoughts in favour of an injured man, though all the powers on earth gainsaid it, to be made the first man in the nation. This position, I know, will ever obstruct my way in the world; and I have conquered my desires accordingly. . . . I do assure you, I do not speak this calmly, after the ill usage in your letter to Addison, out of terror of your wit, or my Lord Treasurer's power; but pure kindness to the agreeable qualities I once so passionately delighted in, in you.[16]

The fact that he had just completed a draft of his letter of resignation no doubt gave him the confidence for this assertion of independence. By the "injured man" he means Marlborough, to whom he again refers in his postscript: "I know no party; but the truth of the question is what I will support as well as I can, when any man I honour is attacked."

Swift replied at once, informing Steele that he is writing an answer simply because he is returning to Ireland and may never see him again. His tone, too, is a bit more restrained than in his previous letters:

In your yesterday's letter, you are pleased to take the complaining side, and think it hard I should write to Mr. Addison as I did, only for an allusion. This allusion was only calling a clergyman of some little distinction an infidel: a clergyman who was your friend, who always loved you, who had endeavoured at least to serve you, and who, whenever he did write anything, made it sacred to himself never to fling out the least hint against you.

Swift then denies, for the third time in the course of this dispute, that he is connected with the *Examiner*. In regard to a specific passage in the Tory paper which Steele had accused him of fathering, he writes, "I never talked or writ to that author in my life, so that he could not have learned it from me. . . ." Much more important, however, is Swift's next point, which goes to the heart of his quarrel with Steele. He asserts that their dispute is not about political principles but personal allegiances:

. . . I think, principles at present are quite out of the case, and that we dispute wholly about persons. In these last you and I differ; but in the other I think, we agree, for I have in print professed myself in politics, to be what we formerly called a Whig.[17]

This statement, of course, is entirely consistent with Swift's repeated descriptions of his position since his alliance with the Oxford ministry. It would be oversimplifying to accept his explanation to Steele with complete literalness; the contrast in their attitudes toward the peace or toward the "monied interest" is sufficient evidence that principles were sometimes involved in their differences. But on other issues, such as "passive obedience" or the Hanoverian Succession, they were apparently in agreement, though led by party allegiances to emphasize different aspects of the questions. Swift seeks in this last letter to Steele to remind him that his political "conversion" in 1710, which resulted in the end of their friendship, had not meant a shift in principles but simply an attachment to a new group of political leaders whose policies he felt to be more in accord with his own convictions than were those of the Junto. Before that time he had regarded himself as unattached to any "party," unlike Steele, who was always a "Whig" not only in principle but in the sense of Swift's definition in the *Examiner*, "one *who believed in the late Ministry*."

This, then, is what Swift means when he writes, "We dispute wholly about persons." As for the specific case of Marlborough, he assures Steele that he has prevented five hundred "hard things" from being said against him, even though he cannot share Steele's high opinion of the Duke. Swift concludes by reminding Steele of the compliment he had paid him in his *Proposal* for correcting the English tongue. Soon after this letter, on June 1, he left for Ireland. The private phase of their quarrel was closed.

It is essential that this sudden outbreak of bitterness between Swift and Steele be seen in its proper perspective. The *Guardian*'s hit at Swift and the subsequent exchange of angry letters were not, as is sometimes implied, the crucial events in the end of Swift's friendship for Steele. That friendship had ceased to exist in any real sense when Swift began moving in Tory circles and writing in support of the Harley government. These incidents of 1713 were merely the climax of an estrangement which had lasted for over two years. During this period, the hostility and ill feeling between the two men had increased in intensity as the result of the gradual accumulation of new grievances and specific points of conflict. Their present quarrel was an almost inevitable result of the pressures which these circumstances had created.

Indeed, unless it is viewed in this way, Steele's sudden onslaught is simply unaccountable, coming as it did in a period when the relations between Whig and Tory writers were extraordinarily cordial. One of the primary issues involved in the quarrel was the Tory treatment of Marlborough, which Miss Blanchard singles out as the dominant factor in the estrangement between Swift and Steele. Her point, as I have already indicated, is probably overstated, but admittedly the question of the Duke was paramount as far as the surface of the present dispute is concerned. Yet Marlborough had been attacked much more severely by the Tory press in the months following his dismissal in 1712, and Steele was then silent, although he must have known that some of the attacks, such as *The Conduct of the Allies,* were by Swift.

Nor will the problem of Swift's authorship of the *Examiner* serve as an explanation. The actual writer of the paper, William Oldisworth, was unknown to Swift personally, although it has been suggested that Swift communicated with him through John Barber, the printer. At this time Oldisworth had been the author of the *Examiner* for a year and a half, and though the larger areas of propaganda were doubtless prescribed from above, "the details of composition must have been left almost entirely in his hands." [18] Steele, it must be remembered, accuses Swift not simply of general supervision and responsibility but of actually writing specific passages. How sincere he was in this accusation is perhaps open to question; as Swift himself points out, one would think that Steele could distinguish his style from Oldisworth's. At any rate, the timing of Steele's charges is again curious. By the time Swift stopped writing the papers in 1711, his share in the *Examiner* was well known to the Opposition. Maynwaring's *Medley* insinuated as much, and Gay's *The Present State of Wit,* with which Steele must have been familiar, listed Swift by name as the author of the Tory paper. But only two years later did Steele directly accuse his former friend of a connection with the *Examiner*. It is difficult to account for his delay, or indeed for the entire quarrel, except in terms of an eruption of bitterness and resentment which had been accumulating since Swift's change of parties in 1710.

2.

During Swift's absence from London, both Addison and Steele entered political controversies arising from the terms of the Treaty of Utrecht. Addison made one of his relatively rare sorties into direct political journalism with the publication in July, 1713, of *The Late Tryal and Conviction of Count Tariff*. In these months, a pamphlet warfare raged over the commercial treaty with France which formed a part of the Tory peace. The agreement called for a freer trade with France at the expense of trade with Portugal, and it was vigorously opposed by the commercial interests which had prospered under the protection of a high tariff. Petitions were circulated from woolen weavers, brandy distillers, silk weavers, representatives of the linen industry, and other trading interests.[19] It was largely as a result of this agitation that the Whigs achieved their first significant parliamentary victory since the change of ministries. On June 18, the tariff clauses of the treaty were defeated in Commons by a narrow majority;

in the voting the Whigs were joined by a number of Tories, the most notable being Sir Thomas Hanmer. Oxford himself gave only lukewarm support to the project, a fact which widened the split between the Lord Treasurer and Bolingbroke; to the latter, the commercial treaty represented the cornerstone of a new foreign policy involving an alliance with France against the Allies.[20] In the press the battle was waged mainly in the pages of Defoe's *Mercator* and its Whig opponent the *British Merchant,* which used the mercantilist theory of the balance of trade as its chief weapon against the treaty. Steele, later in the year, entered the controversy with a long paper in the *Guardian* (No. 170 for September 25) based on the *General Maxims in Trade* which Sir Theodore Janssen, one of Defoe's antagonists, had contributed to the *British Merchant.*

Addison's contribution to the Whig cause in this instance took the form of a light political allegory. The parliamentary defeat of the tariff provisions of the treaty is represented as a trial in which the defendant Count Tariff, an arrogant Francophile, is charged with crimes against the plaintiff Goodman Fact, an honest, outspoken Englishman. "Fact" is supported in court by thousands of weavers, clothiers, distillers, drapers, planters, merchants, and the like. More interesting, though, are the witnesses who appear in defense of the Count. They include the worthless Spaniard Don Assiento (the Tories claimed that an advantage to be gained by their treaty was the *assiento,* or South American slave trade); the *Mercator,* a "false, shuffling, prevaricating rascal"; and the *Examiner.* The last is described as a notorious knight who was hired to testify whenever necessary. Addison continues:

> This was the EXAMINER; a person who had abused almost every man in *England,* that deserved well of his country. . . . It was allowed by every body, that so foul-mouthed a witness never appeared in any cause. Seeing several persons of great eminence, who had maintained the cause of Goodman *Fact,* he called them ideots, blockheads, villains, knaves, infidels, atheists, apostates, fiends, and devils: never did man show so much eloquence in ribaldry.[21]

After his testimony the court declares in favor of Goodman Fact, amid general rejoicing in the city of London. It is interesting that Addison should launch an attack on the *Examiner* just a month after the quarrel between Swift and Steele, in which the degree of Swift's responsibility for the Tory journal had been a burning issue. The *Examiner*'s general position on the Peace gave some warrant for introducing it into an indictment of the commercial treaty, but, as that paper itself truthfully protested, it "never yet touch'd upon that subject," the ministerial defense being conducted entirely by Defoe's *Mercator*.

Addison's satiric parable is clever and effective, his basic device permitting him to make serious charges while preserving his playful tone. One of his best touches of this sort is the Count's accusation that the plaintiff's name is not Fact but Faction:

> The Count was so pleased with this conceit, that for an hour together he repeated it in every sentence; calling his antagonist's assertions, the reports of faction; his friends, the sons of faction; the testimonies of his witnesses, the dictates of faction: nay, with such a degree of impudence did he push this matter, that when he heard the cries of above a million of people begging for their bread, he termed the prayers and importunities of such a starving multitude, the CLAMOURS OF FACTION.[22]

Such an exposure of a favorite Tory device was difficult to answer, and Addison's pamphlet met with little criticism. The *Examiner* contented itself with a brief summary, followed by the rather inept rejoinder, "Passages of this extraordinary Nature are what the *Whigs* call *Answering, Replying, Vindicating,* &c. . . ." [23] A month later Defoe attempted to employ Addison's method in defense of the treaty by publishing *Memoirs of Count Tariff*, advertised in the *Examiner* for August 21. And it is worth noting that Pope, two years later, includes Addison's piece in his *Key to the Lock* as an example of the new custom of venting "political Spleen" in allegory and fable: ". . . if a Treasurer is to be glanced at, an *Ant* with a *white Straw* is introduced; if a Treaty of Commerce is to be ridiculed, 'tis immediately metamorphosed into a Tale of Count *Tariff*." [24]

Although Addison was willing at this time to engage in political controversy in this anonymously published pamphlet, he was more circumspect in the *Guardian,* which he directed from July 1 to August 3. None of the essays in that period could have offended on the score of politics. When Steele resumed control of the paper, however, matters took a different turn. On August 7, 1713, Steele suddenly entered another political quarrel arising from the provisions of the Treaty of Utrecht, in this case a controversy over the demolition of the port of Dunkirk. By the terms of the treaty France was to destroy the harbor and fortifications, but the Whigs distrusted the sincerity of their intentions in this matter. The destruction of Dunkirk seemed essential to them, since they considered the port a threat to England's security and trade as well as a possible point of origin for a Jacobite invasion. Their suspicions were increased when M. Tugghe, representing the magistrates of Dunkirk, circulated a memorial asking that the harbor be spared. Steele's *Guardian* No. 128 (August 7) purports to be a letter to Nestor Ironside from an "English Tory" protesting Tugghe's petition. Here Steele states in summary fashion the Whig arguments for the destruction of the port: the demolition is the "most material part" of the peace treaty, Dunkirk is a menace to English trade and military security, from this port the Pretender sailed to Scotland, the Dutch were induced to sign the peace treaty only because they expected its demolition, and its destruction would remove the danger of future French attack from Dunkirk to Brest. Three times Steele repeats the statement, "The British Nation expect the immediate demolition of Dunkirk." In his paper of August 11, Steele returns to the subject of Dunkirk, restating two paragraphs from No. 128 in the guise of making a correction.[25]

The Tories were quick to seize upon Steele's most vulnerable point in their furious replies to the *Guardian*. His phrase "the British Nation expect" was interpreted as an insolent reminder to the Queen herself and consequently as a direct attack upon the royal prerogative. The *Examiner* replied:

I say *it is not so;* the *British* Nation does not EXPECT that Her Majesty should divest Her Self of the Power which is in Her Hands, by the Possession of *Dunkirk,* to do Her Self Right, and to secure to Her Self the Performance of such Conditions from all the Princes concerned, as they have agreed to be just and ought to be performed; but which we do not find them so free to execute, as the Obligations *Britain* has laid on them has given us reason to expect.[26]

He goes on to develop this point, suggesting that England needs protection against the Dutch as well as the French. The *Examiner* also loosed a tirade of personal invective against Steele, accusing him of ingratitude, of insulting his Prince "while he is eating Her Bread." Oldisworth was thus either unaware that Steele had resigned his government post or deliberately chose to ignore that fact. He ridicules the Whigs for making Steele their favorite now that he has "let them know that he durst assault his Queen" and suggests that Steele will be expelled from Parliament if his election should prove successful.

One of the reasons for the intensity of the Tory reaction to *Guardian* No. 128 was that the ministers themselves were disturbed by the state of affairs at Dunkirk and disliked being reminded of the French failure to carry out the obligations of the treaty.[27] Moreover, it was quite clear that Steele's paper, though ostensibly an answer to Tugghe's memorial, was in reality an attack on the ministry and the validity of the peace which the government had secured. The Tories also professed to believe that it constituted an affront to the prerogative, and this fact, coupled with Steele's variations on the familiar Whig themes of injury to trade and the threat of Jacobitism, made it a piece of Opposition propaganda which extended in significance beyond the immediate issue of Dunkirk.

The campaign against Steele, therefore, was not confined simply to the *Examiner* but extended to separate pamphlets, of which the most notable was *The Honour and Prerogative of the Queen's Majesty Vindicated and Defended Against the Unexampled Insolence of the Author of the Guardian.* The writer makes the usual personal charge of Steele's ingratitude, but, as its title indicates, his pamphlet emphasizes primarily Steele's "affront" to the prerogative. He points out that the English believe in a just balance between the rights of the people and the royal prerogative, and the right of making peace, as well as the terms of the peace, is the "undoubted Prerogative of the Sovereign." On the other side, of course, pamphlets were written in Steele's defense. One of them, *Dunkirk or Dover,* was by the "free-thinking" John Toland, whom the *Examiner* characterized as "a worthy Advocate for such a Man and such a Cause." Oldisworth continues, "He was once the *Butt* of the *Tatler*, but now in high Favour with Mr. *Steele*, and honour'd by him with the Name of *Second*." [28]

Since Steele was already preparing a separate pamphlet to answer his critics, the *Guardian* was kept free of politics for the time being. Most of the papers were again written by Addison, who made the ironic confession, "I write with fear and trembling, ever since that ingenious person the *Examiner* . . . found out treason in the word *expect*." On September 23, in *Guardian* No. 168, Steele announced the publication of his pamphlet on Dunkirk, at the same time reviewing the war of pamphlets which his original letter had provoked. Of his new work he remarks, " 'There are very many scurrilous things said against me, but I have turned them to my advantage, by quoting them at large, and by that means swelling the volume to 1s. price.' " [29]

Steele's work is called *The Importance of Dunkirk Consider'd: In Defence of the Guardian of August the 7th. In a Letter to the Bailiff of Stockbridge;* it was from the borough of Stockbridge that he had been returned to Parliament on August 25. It is a rambling, discursive tract which has, in fact, been "swelled" by the reprinting of earlier pamphlets in the controversy, including Tugghe's memorial, Steele's own letter to the *Guardian*, two pages from a Tory pamphlet, and selected passages from the *Examiner*. Steele, seeking here to provide a detailed answer to his opponents, does not really make any new points about the Dunkirk affair. His arguments for the most part are simply extensions of those in *Guardian* No. 128. There are a few remarks in this tract, however, which may have some relevance to his recent quarrel with Swift. Throughout, for example, Steele hits at the "prostitute Pens" employed in writing for the government, whose behavior constitutes a "Disgrace to Literature." The prerogative and honor of the Crown, he points out, cannot be harmed by the acts of one private individual, who is punishable by law; the real danger arises from unrestrained slander in political pamphlets:

> . . . but true and real Danger to the Queen's Honour may arise, if Persons in Authority Tolerate Men (who have no Compunction of Conscience) in abusing such Instruments of Glory and Honour to our Country as the Illustrious Duke of *Marlborough*, such wise

and faithful Managers as the late Earl of *Godolphin,* such Pious, Disinterested, Generous, and Self-denying Patriots as the Bishops.

It is possible, too, that his comment about one of the pamphlets attacking him may have been directed at Swift. The Tory *Reasons concerning the Immediate Demolishing of Dunkirk* had spoken of Steele's "exquisite Politicks." Steele comments: "He grows in Jest here at last, for he knows as well as I do, that I am no great Politician, and I know what he is, perhaps, a little better than he Thinks. But I shall treat him as the Man whom I suppose him to be, tho' he has not me, as the Man he knows me to be." [30]

If Steele actually believed Swift to be the author of this pamphlet or of any of the many attacks which had appeared against him, he was premature. Swift was indeed to confound Steele very shortly with one of his most devastating satires, but he took no part in the early stages of the controversy over Dunkirk. He had returned to London in the first week of September and had found the Court thrown into confusion by the increasing hostility between Oxford and Bolingbroke. Though still somewhat chagrined by the unwillingness of the ministers to make use of his *History of the Four Last Years of the Queen,* as it was later called, he did not hesitate to leave Ireland with the hope that his "endeavours to reconcile" might avert a ministerial crisis. When he arrived in England, he found that Richard Steele, with whom he had quarreled bitterly just before leaving for Ireland, was now a member of Parliament and had emerged as a leading Whig propagandist as a result of the Dunkirk affair. Moreover, on October 1, Steele dropped the *Guardian* in favor of a new periodical, the *Englishman,* which was to concern itself entirely with political matters. Having once decided to devote his energies almost exclusively to the Whig cause, he appears to have assumed his new role with extraordinary vigor and determination. He was now a prime object of attack in the Tory press, and there is some evidence that even at this early date the Tories had decided to seek his expulsion from the House.[31] Addison was apprehensive about the new course which Steele had set for himself: "I am in a thousand troubles for poor Dick, and wish that his zeal for the public may not be ruinous to himself; but he has sent me word that he is determined to go on, and that any advice I can give him in this particular, will have no weight with him." [32]

Obviously, as the most powerful journalist writing for the government, Swift was now in a position which required him to launch a full-scale attack on Steele for the first time since his alliance with the Oxford ministry. *The Importance of Dunkirk* was dangerous propaganda and had to be answered effectively. Yet it has always been tempting to see Swift's reply, *The Importance of the Guardian Considered,* as motivated primarily by personal animus, as the natural outgrowth of their private quarrel. It is, to be sure, impossible to "prove" that personal feeling played a relatively minor part in Swift's attack, but certain elements in the background of his satire make it appear not so much the result of bitterness toward Steele the individual as the product of a sincere difference in convictions and of the exigencies of an immediate political situation. In the first place, the Tory charge that Steele had affronted the royal prerogative was not a mere expedient of pamphlet warfare. Their philosophy of government—especially Bolingbroke's—encouraged the view that an attack on the policies of the Queen's ministers was an attack on the Queen.[33] That Swift to some extent shared this attitude is indicated by a passage in a letter to Archbishop King, where he discusses popular objections to the Treaty of Peace:

> We have been forced to conceal the best side, which I agree has been unfortunate and unpopular; but you will please to consider that this way of every subject interposing their sentiments upon the management of foreign negotiations, is a very new thing among us; and the suffering it has been thought, in the opinion of wise men, too great a strain upon the prerogative. . . .[34]

On this ground, then, Swift may have been sincere in his objections to Steele's famous phrase, "The British Nation expect the immediate demolition of Dunkirk." Even aside from the fact that Steele's writings about Dunkirk, and the agitation which they had aroused, posed a threat to the interests of Swift's "party" which he could hardly ignore, his disapproval of the underlying principle of Steele's position might have prompted him to a reply.

Furthermore, during the month and a half interval between the publication of Steele's pamphlet and Swift's reply, allusions to Swift in the press of both sides made it increasingly difficult for him to avoid the role of Steele's antagonist, even if he had wished to do so. Their private quarrel was rapidly becoming more public. On October 2, the *Examiner* answered Steele's book, and in the course of its detailed attack the following remark occurred: "I know of no Person yet named for the *Examiner*, to whom Mr. *Steele* is not obliged, as a *Wit*; or who has not try'd to reform both his *Morals* and *Politicks*." [35] Four days later, in the first issue of the *Englishman*, Steele replied to this charge in a letter addressed to Oxford. With obvious reference to Swift, he writes: "My Lord, your Rogue has me safe here; I cannot answer to this, without naming a witty Man or two with whom I have passed some agreeable Hours; for which I have too much Gratitude to name them under Suspicion of Accomplices with the *Examiner*. . . ." As Miss Blanchard points out, Steele, despite this ironic disclaimer, was convinced that Swift was responsible for the *Examiner*'s attacks on him at this period; and it is possible that he meant a passage such as the following to be applied directly to his old friend:

> Your Man, My Lord, would be in the Right of this, if I esteemed Men for the Faculties of the Head, and not the Inclinations of the Heart. I never said, My Lord, but that your Man was fit for much better Business than that in which he is employed, had it pleased God to have given him Grace; but as he has used his Wit, he appears the Worst Man that ever had the Education of a Gentleman; and I cannot recollect one Paper, in which, I believe, he has not acted against the Conviction of his Conscience.[36]

Again, the *Examiner* for October 12 ridicules Steele in a letter to "Jacob Kit-Cat, Bookseller" from "John Smith, Corn-cutter," a figure from the *Tatler;* here, too, Steele fancied he saw Swift's hand at work, and "Smith" has a series of letters in the *Englishman* demanding that the Tory writer drop his mask of anonymity. Finally, the *Examiner* for October 16, in reviewing correspondence which has been received relating to Steele, cites a communication from a "correspondent" who, I think, is clearly meant to suggest Swift:

> A Third Correspondent, who will not let me do my self the Honour to mention him, writes to me in his own Name, and in the

Name of a great Number of witty and learned Tories; on whose
Behalf he acquaints me, that I need not consider Mr. *Steele,* as a
Tartar does his Enemy whom I am to kill for Selfish Reasons, that
I may thereby come in for his *Assets* of Wit, Learning and El-
oquence: *For,* says he, very handsomely, *you will be no great
Gainer by the* Demise. He rather presses me to accept of the Offer
made by himself and Friends, who have agreed to make over to me
all the *Tatlers, Spectators,* and *Guardians,* written by that Party,
of which a complete List is shortly to come out. . . . I my self,
says this worthy Creature, wrote the *Spectator,* which begins thus;
Censure, says a late Ingenious Writer, *is the Tax a Man pays to the
Publick, for being Eminent;* but I little thought, adds he, that ever
Mr. *Steele* would be employ'd to *Collect* that *Tax* for the *Publick,*
and approve himself, what he never was before, so very good a
Paymaster.[37]

The *Spectator* referred to, No. 101 for June 26, 1711, is actually
by Addison, but the quotation which begins the essay is from
Swift's *Thoughts on Various Subjects.* And the entire passage is
meant to recall Steele's intimacy with Tory writers and the extent to which he was obligated to Swift, in particular, for his
"wit."

For a month before the publication of Swift's attack on Steele,
then, their personal differences were a subject of comment in the
party journals. On November 2, his satire finally appeared, entitled *The Importance of the Guardian Considered, in a Second
Letter to the Bailiff of Stockbridge. By a Friend of Mr. St—le.*
It is in no sense intended as an "answer" to Steele's arguments:
in his Preface Swift announces that he has entered very little
into the subject of Steele's pamphlet but has considered it simply
as a critic and commentator. In other words his reply is to be
frankly *ad hominem,* on the principle he has so beautifully
enunciated elsewhere, that although a book may not be intrin-
sically better or worse according to the nature of its author, "yet
when it happens to make a Noise, we are apt and curious, as in
other Noises, to look about from whence it cometh." [38] And he
states at the outset the premise which is to justify the application
of that principle in this instance: *"The Importance of Dunkirk,
is chiefly taken up in shewing you the Importance of Mr.
Steele. . . ."* [39]

But even though personal ridicule is the only goal which this piece sets for itself, it is seldom allowed to degenerate into mere abuse. Swift employs, as usual, a variety of techniques to achieve indirection, from simple irony to hyperbole. His central ironic device is to pose as the explicator, the commentator, who is patiently explaining Mr. Steele's nonsense to the Bailiff of Stockbridge, since that gentleman of the country is unfamiliar with the subtleties of "London-writers." As the satire moves along, however, this ironic framework becomes less important, though it is reasserted in the final paragraph. As is often the case with Swift, the mechanically conceived "mask" so favored by modern critics will not quite fit here; instead of the "explicator" he becomes, when it suits his purpose, simply the "answerer" or the "accuser," and the irony is deliberately broken by direct statement. The complex effect of the satire arises partly from this very shifting of styles, from suddenly dropping the ironic pose in favor of straightforward, indignant criticism spoken *in propria persona.*

Swift traces for the Bailiff Steele's career from his days as *publisher* (not writer) of the *Tatler* and *Spectator* to his entrance into the dispute over Dunkirk, toward which the Whig attitude is depicted as completely inconsistent and molded to fit political expediency. Then, one by one, various aspects of both Steele's pamphlet and his character are subjected to Swift's irony. For example, Steele had answered the Tory charge of ingratitude, of insulting the Queen while he was eating her bread, by pointing out that he had resigned his government offices before entering the controversy. Consequently, writes Swift, "the *Bread was eaten* at least a Week before he would offer to *insult his Prince:* So that the Folly of the Examiner's objecting Ingratitude to him upon this Article, is manifest to all the World." Again, Swift, when defending the principle that it is more criminal to reflect on a majority in power than a minority out of power, suddenly introduces Steele's notoriety as a debtor: "What Bailiff would venture to Arrest Mr. *Steele,* now he has the Honour to be your Representative? and what Bailiff ever scrupled it before?" He is careful, however, to admit that Steele has certain merits, in each case qualifying the virtue almost out of existence; Steele has indeed acquired the reputation of a wit (through his intimacy with Addison) and has, it must be confessed, a talent for humor (after the first bottle). To attack the style of his opponent, Swift uses his customary mock encomium, though in the later section of the satire he is less ironic, accusing Steele directly of "studying Cadence instead of Propriety, and filling up Nitches with Words before he has adjusted his Conceptions to them." [40] In the last pages of *The Importance of Dunkirk*, Steele, with his usual self-righteousness, had described at some length the "Charity" which motivated him, thus making himself an obvious target for the kind of satire Swift is writing here. Accordingly, Swift the "explicator" informs the Bailiff that Steele's entire pamphlet was written simply for the sake of these "exalted Strains of Piety and Resignation." This "miraculous and sudden Reformation" becomes the lever for introducing the sins of Steele's youth, which Swift had earlier promised to ignore.

It should be noted that although Swift's arguments are all *ad hominem*, certain facets of the Dunkirk question are carefully introduced. The insinuation is made several times, for instance, that the Whigs themselves are responsible for the circulation of Tugghe's petition. More important, within the framework of personal ridicule there emerges the question of Steele's "attack" upon the royal prerogative. It is treated ironically in the form of two "letters," one from Steele to the Queen and the other a reply. In the first, Steele complains that the port has not been demolished, that Oxford and Bolingbroke clearly intend to use it for bringing in the Pretender, and that the nation "EXPECTS" its destruction. The Queen's answer emphasizes Steele's insolence: *"I do not conceive that any of your Titles empower you to be my Director, or to report to me the Expectations of my People."* Elsewhere, the issue of the prerogative, which is perhaps at the heart of Swift's disapproval of Steele's position, is considered with more directness. What right, asks Swift, has an individual such as Steele, "in his *Tatling* or *Pamphleteering* Capacity," to fix the ordinary rules of government? He complains that Steele's definition of "prerogative" has made the concept meaningless, since it is not to be trusted with the Queen as an individual and since the ministers, in Steele's view, may not act by its authority: "He tells you, *The Prerogative attends the Crown;* and therefore, I suppose, must lie in the *Tower* to be shewn for Twelve pence, but never produced, except at a Coronation, or passing an Act." [41]

The Importance of the Guardian, in the opinion of the *Examiner,* "seems to *Tickle* rather than *Wound,*" but there can be little doubt that Steele was greatly offended by Swift's satire. On the same day that the Tory attack appeared, *Examiner* No. 43 made a general indictment of the Whig leaders Marlborough, Godolphin, Walpole, and, especially, Wharton. Steele appears to have attributed both this *Examiner* and the *Importance* to Swift, and *Englishman* No. 13 (November 3) is a bitter invective against the Tory paper, accusing its author of belonging to neither party but of being a complete renegade. Four days later Steele again issued a warning to his opponent: "As fast as that Slanderer endeavours to make those whom I wish well odious, I shall labour to make those whom he celebrates ridiculous." [42]

During the remainder of November the war between Steele and the *Examiner* continued at a furious pace. Nearly every issue of the Tory paper attacked Steele personally, and inevitably the charges duplicated those laid to Steele in Swift's pamphlet. No. 45, for example, contains the remark, "I wrote *Spectators* and *Tatlers* when he only published them," to which Steele promptly replied, "as soon as some People can lay hold of him, his next Lucubration will be in the *Round-house.*" [43] Meanwhile, other Whig pamphlets were busily attacking the new Dean, and almost all assume, like Steele, that he is still the editor of the *Examiner.* Abel Boyer, for example, makes the charge in his *Political State* for November, where he prints Swift's *Part of the Seventh Epistle of the First Book of Horace Imitated* and turns it against its author. Lines of self-description like "In State-Opinions *a-la Mode*" were obviously well suited to the needs of a Whig writer who wished to ridicule Swift.

In November, too, appeared a pamphlet entitled *Two Letters concerning the Author of the Examiner,* which praises Steele and indicts Swift. The chief object of attack is the *Examiner,* the author of which wears many clothes but is "never so learned and so witty as when he wears the Cassock." The Tory ministers are ironically defended from the charge that they encourage such a writer; they are too well known for their love of learning to be pleased with his invectives against Steele, "whose Writings and Publications . . . have contributed more to the refining and amending of the Nation, than any Man's that ever went before him." [44]

Such Whig defenses of Steele, however, were no match for the virulent attacks of the Tories, who intensely resented Steele's growing prominence as a propagandist. One of the most important of these pamphlets was *The Character of Richard Steele, Esq.*, signed "Toby, Abel's Kinsman," but written by William Wagstaffe. It was published on November 14, 1713, and was later reprinted in Wagstaffe's *Works* (1726), where an anonymous memoir prefixed to the volume states that Steele was personally unknown to Wagstaffe. This fact, if true, makes the *Character* a doubly curious performance, for its tone is unusually abusive. No effort is made to achieve any sort of ironic detachment; Wagstaffe contents himself throughout with direct criticism of the most scathing and malicious sort. Like Swift, he charges that Steele's wit is made up of "borrowed colours," that his literary reputation has been gained by publishing the work of his more talented friends. His career as a politician was instigated by the Whig poets at Button's coffeehouse, though he needed little encouragement to stand for Parliament, since his wit and credit were running low. At this point, writes Wagstaffe, "the *Political Cacoethes* began to break out upon him with greater Violence, because it had been suppressed, and He, who had lived so long upon the *Lucubrations* of others, was resolv'd at last to do Something." [45] In answer to *The Importance of Dunkirk*, the usual charges of insolence and ingratitude are made, with particular attention given to Steele's reflections on Harley, who, it is said, was alone responsible for his continuation in the Stamp Office for three years. Wagstaffe makes no attempt to consider the political issues involved in the Dunkirk controversy, aside from the casual assurance that the port is being demolished and the accusation that the Whigs "expect" its demolition "from a particular Care of the *Dutch Trade*."

Throughout, Steele is considered as the archhypocrite who preaches benevolence and charity but whose own character is not animated by those principles. He has contracted his many debts through luxury and vanity, his dabbling in alchemy and other projects is pernicious to the public, he has taken bribes, and in the *Tatler* he was willing to *"Pimp* in Print." After this recital, Wagstaffe's tone becomes even more severe:

> . . . it raises the Contempt and Indignation of every honest Man, to hear a Person of the vilest Principles, and the most mercenary Hireling who ever prostituted his Pen in the Defence of any Faction, giving himself such an Air of Sanctity and Virtue.[46]

A "Postscript" to the *Character* quotes several passages from Steele and ridicules their style and bad grammar.

Oddly enough, there is no allusion to Swift in this pamphlet, even in contexts where a reference to his connection with Steele would definitely be expected. This omission, together with a great deal of other circumstantial evidence, was used by C. W. Dilke in his effort to add this piece to Swift's canon; only recently have his arguments been convincingly refuted.[47] In his own day, Swift was consistently accused of having written this *Character* of his old friend. Teerink lists an "answer" which clearly hints that Swift is the author of the original piece. The same accusation was made in 1714 in *Essays Divine, Moral and Political,* an equally vicious attack upon Swift, and many years later in Jonathan Smedley's *Gulliveriana.* More important, Steele himself was convinced that Swift had written the pamphlet, a fact which reveals well enough the present state of their relations. In *Englishman* No. 57 (February 15, 1713/14) he discussed the attack and its author:

> I think I know the Author of this, and to shew him I know no Revenge but in the method of heaping Coals on his head by Benefits, I forbear giving him what he deserves; for no other reason, but that I know his Sensibility of Reproach is such, as that he would be unable to bear Life it self under half the ill Language he has given me.[48]

While Swift and Steele were engaging publicly in recriminations of this sort, political warfare was having its effect in the literary world in a manner more subtle but no less invidious. Addison was now well established in Button's coffeehouse with his "little senate" of Whig literary men; in addition, he may have succeeded Maynwaring, now dead, as the unofficial supervisor of party writing.[49] He and Steele were now active not only

in the Kit-Kat Club but in the smaller Whig group known as
the Hanover Club, of which Ambrose Philips was secretary. As
marshall of these Whig literary forces, Addison, in the winter of
1713/14, made a concerted effort to prevent Pope from aligning
himself with Swift and his circle of Tory writers. Some of the details of that incident are worth mentioning briefly, for they illustrate very clearly the manner in which the pattern of literary
rivalries was influenced and determined by that of political allegiances.

In 1712 Pope had been cordially received by Addison and
Steele, and in the following year, as a contributor to the *Guardian,*
he continued on friendly terms with most of the Whig wits. Toward the end of 1713, however, he became increasingly restive
in the society at Button's. His ridicule of Philips in *Guardian* No.
40 made enemies for him among the minor Whigs, and his growing association with Swift and the Tories was a matter of concern to Addison, who wrote in November advising him not to
content himself with half the nation for his admirers when he
might command them all. His enemies later accused Pope of
having been both a Whig and a Tory at this time, of having
written *Guardians* and *Examiners* simultaneously. In reality,
however, he was little moved by the political issues which were
debated so passionately by Swift and Steele; his motives in abandoning the Whigs were more personal and literary. Not the least
of these, as Professor Sherburn points out, was his dissatisfaction
with the restricted literary interests of the *Spectator* tradition,
for he was outgrowing those who would "fair-sex it till the
world's end." [50]

In October of 1713, Pope approached Swift with a plan for
satirizing follies in learning by a burlesque monthly periodical,
a proposal which was to lead within a few months to the formation of the famous Scriblerus Club.[51] At first Pope hoped to
gather both Whig and Tory writers to support his scheme, and
he apparently broached the matter to Addison, whose response
was noncommittal. Though he feared losing Pope to the Tories,
satire of this kind was not to his taste, and his position as the
leading Whig journalist would make it undesirable for him to
indulge in prolonged attacks on Grub Street. From the Tories,
however, especially Swift, Pope's plan met with unqualified en-

thusiasm. Aside from the literary predilections which prompted his support, Swift was not likely to miss this chance of winning both Gay and Pope away from the Addison-Steele group. By February, 1713/14, Pope's project had taken the form of a small club of Tories, including Swift, Pope, Parnell, Gay, Arbuthnot, and the Earl of Oxford, and its design now involved a more complicated scheme for satirizing the follies of all fields of learning.

The formation of the Scriblerus Club meant that Addison and his group no longer commanded the greatest prestige in literary circles. The Whigs made no secret of their resentment of Pope's alignment with the Tories. Pope wrote later that he had been accused by Philips of entering into a "Cabal with Dean *Swift* and others to write against the *Whig-Interest,* and in particular to undermine his own reputation, and that of his friends *Steel* and *Addison.*" And after the death of the Queen, Jervas wrote to Pope, "he [Addison] was afraid Dr. *Swift* might have carry'd you too far among the enemy during the heat of the animosity." [52] Jealousy of this sort, then, must be added to the political differences which exacerbated relations between Addison and Swift. The literary world was split along party lines, and it was difficult for a writer of talent to avoid making a choice between the groups dominated by these two figures. Even a poet like Pope who wished to remain neutral found the task insuperable in the violent political atmosphere of 1713/14.

3.

We are now in a position to examine the climactic development in the public duel between Swift and Steele, their bitter controversy over the Protestant Succession. As the leading spokesman for the Whigs, Steele sought to prove, in a pamphlet called *The Crisis,* that the Succession was endangered by the machinations of the Oxford ministry. As the chief Tory propagandist, it naturally fell upon Swift to answer him. But this new quarrel actually began even before *The Crisis* could appear, for in the weeks prior to its publication we find Swift busily satirizing both Steele's preparations for his tract and Whig alarmism in general. At the same time, the *Examiner* and Steele's *Englishman* continued to do battle on a variety of other issues, some of which again touched the personal differences between Steele and Swift.

The political struggle which lay behind this paper warfare was intensified by the serious illness of the Queen at Christmas, 1713. Although she quickly recovered, her illness threw into relief all the problems and confusion which surrounded the issue of the Succession. The Whigs were united more than ever by their conviction that the ministers sought a Stuart Restoration, while the Tories were hopelessly split, not only by the struggle between the Lord Treasurer and the Secretary, but also by the increasing prominence of the Hanover Tories or "Whimsicals," led by Sir Thomas Hanmer. Neither Oxford nor Bolingbroke had any settled course to follow; their correspondence with the Pretender was exploratory and expedient, dictated by the necessity of insuring the safety of their own position in any turn of events. They demanded that the Pretender change his religion, and his refusal threw them into even greater consternation. Nor were they the only ones playing a double game; in February, Marlborough simultaneously assured the Hanoverian Elector of his loyalty and asked for a pardon at the court of the Pretender.[53] The position of the Tory ministers, with no real policy to guide them, grew dangerously weak. Only by twelve votes were they able to defeat a motion in Lords that the Succession was in danger under their administration. In actuality, there was little chance that a Restoration could occur. Louis XIV, still at war with the Emperor, could not have spared an army for such a purpose, and it was the combination of France, the Pretender, and the Tories that the Whigs feared.[54] Nevertheless, agitation over the question was naturally intense, and a deluge of pamphlets proclaimed the imminent danger of popery and the Pretender.

Though well aware of the dissensions among the Tories, Swift seems never to have doubted the safety of the Protestant Succession. There is no evidence that he knew of the ministers' flirtation with James. In his eyes the protests and accusations of Steele and other Whig writers were deliberately alarmist, the "Clamours of a Faction" seeking to exploit popular fears and superstitions as a weapon against the government. Consequently, when Bishop Burnet pressed the Whig charges in an *Introduction* to a work to be published later, the third volume of his

History of the Reformation of the Church of England, Swift
recognized the political purpose of issuing this *Introduction*
separately and wrote a witty, detailed reply. His answer, entitled *A Preface to the B—p of S-r-m's Introduction,* appeared on
December 7, 1713, signed "Gregory Misosarum." Here Swift sets
out to show that the "crisis" over the Succession is a manufactured political issue. The Bishop writes "as if Destruction hung
over us by a single Hair; as if the *Pope,* the *Devil,* the *Pretender,*
and *France,* were just at our Doors"—an opinion which it is very
convenient for the "present Designs" of the Whigs to spread.
It is true, Swift says, that when the Bishop first undertook his
History, there was real cause for alarm, since a Popish plot was
afoot, the presumptive heir to the Crown was a papist, and Louis
XIV at the height of his power. In the present case, however,
the Pretender is excluded forever by acts of Parliament and ab-
jured by all persons in employment, the heir and his family are
Protestants, and the King of France is at his lowest ebb. The
Bishop, it appears, "hath been poring so long upon *Fox's* Book
of Martyrs, that he imagines himself living in the Reign of Queen
Mary, and is resolved to set up for a *Knight-Errant* against
Popery." [55]

It is unnecessary to analyze Swift's pamphlet in detail, but it
should be noted that everything which is said about Burnet's
alarmism is meant to apply to Steele and his *Englishman.* Swift
makes the equation at the beginning of his *Preface* and reasserts it at appropriate moments throughout. In the first paragraph he observes that Steele, in the *Englishman,* seems almost
to have transcribed the Bishop's opinions; "These Notions," he
adds, "I take to have been dictated by the same Masters, leaving
to each Writer that peculiar Manner of expressing himself, which
the Poverty of our Language forceth me to call their Stile." [56]
As Miss Blanchard points out, Swift has in mind especially *Englishman* No. 14, published on Guy Fawkes day, where Steele,
like Burnet, writes as if popery threatened England at any moment and where he quotes in his support excerpts from a sermon
by Swift's friend St. George Ashe.[57] Swift, at any rate, makes the
most of his device of drawing Steele into his attack on Burnet. He
depicts both as agents in the "grand Preparations" which the
Whigs are making against the next Parliamentary session, a

design he first got wind of when "the *Guardian* changed his Title, and professed to engage in Faction." At another point in his satire he reiterates the connections, both in subject matter and style, between Steele and Burnet. And he writes a mock defense of Steele and the Whigs against Burnet's reproof that they are insufficiently aroused to the present danger:

> With due Submission to the profound Sagacity of this Prelate, who can smell *Popery* at five hundred Miles distance, better than *Fanaticism* just under his Nose; I take Leave to tell him, that this Reproof to his Friends, for want of Zeal and Clamour against Popery, Slavery, and the *Pretender,* is what they have not deserved. Are the Pamphlets and Papers daily published by the sublime Authors of his Party, full of any Thing else? Are not the QUEEN, the Ministers, the Majority of Lords and Commons, loudly taxed in print with this Charge against them at full Length? Is it not the perpetual Eccho of every Whig Coffee-House and Club? Have they not quartered *Popery* and the *Pretender* upon the Peace and Treaty of Commerce; upon the possessing, and quitting, and keeping, and demolishing of *Dunkirk?* . . . Can mortal Man do more? To deal plainly, my Lord, your Friends are not strong enough *yet* to make an Insurrection, and it is unreasonable to expect one from them, until their Neighbours be ready.[58]

One of the most important pamphlets in this flood of Whig propaganda was to be Steele's *Crisis,* for which elaborate advertisements had been appearing since October. Well before the work itself finally appeared, Swift satirized its author and its design in *The First Ode of the Second Book of Horace Paraphras'd: And Address'd to Richard St—le, Esq.,* an octosyllabic poem published on January 7, 1713/14. In some of his best satiric verses Swift ridicules Steele's projected volume by predicting that it will consist simply of the old Whig themes in elaborate dress. The Peace will be railed at, Oxford will be attacked, the creation of twelve peers (without Steele's permission) will be deplored, and dangerous *"Leagues* among the Great" will be revealed. As for the "danger" to the Succession, Swift dismisses it at the beginning of his poem; Steele, he says, will simply tell us what everyone already knows, that Anne will be succeeded by the Elector of Hanover. Again he connects Steele and Burnet:

> *Dick,* thour't resolv'd, as I am told,
> Some strange *Arcana* to unfold,
> And with the help of *Buckley's* Pen
> To vamp the *good Old Cause* again,
> Which thou (such *Bur—t's* shrewd Advice is)
> Must furbish up and Nickname *CRISIS.*
> Thou pompously wilt let us know
> What all the World knew long ago, . . .
> That we a *German* Prince must own
> When *A—N* for Heav'n resigns Her Throne.[59]

Swift's tone, throughout, is pointedly condescending and patronizing. Steele, he says, is simply unfit for meddling with state affairs and writing political satires: "For Madmen, Children, Wits and Fools / Shou'd never meddle with Edg'd Tools." Instead, Steele is advised to restrict himself to his usual business of "trudging in a beaten Track" and immortalizing our *"Dolls and Jenneys"* with Philips, Dennis, and D'Urfey. Steele's style is mocked, in a passage clearly parodying *Englishman* No. 14, and his new career in Commons is ridiculed in a "vision" of him pompously entering Parliament. His earlier, successful days as writer of the *Tatler* are contrasted with his political career, which Swift consistently belittles with an amused air of contemptuous superiority.

During the period when *The Crisis* was in preparation, Steele's *Englishman* continued to antagonize the Tories by its running feud with the *Examiner.* According to Miss Blanchard, Steele was convinced that Swift was in charge of the Tory paper this winter and the actual writer of papers satirizing Steele himself.[60] Most of the specific issues about which the two papers clashed need not concern us here, but a few which attracted Swift's attention may be mentioned. The *Examiner* and other government papers had accused the Whigs of joyfully spreading the report that the Queen had died during her illness at Christmas. Steele, in *Englishman* No. 43, answered these charges and accused the Tories of flippancy in their treatment of her recovery. Then, with the help of Swift, Mrs. Manley gave the Tory version in *A Modest Enquiry into the Reasons of the Joy Expressed by a Certain Sett of People, upon the Spreading of a Report of Her*

Majesty's Death. She describes, first, the imaginary reaction of a foreigner puzzled by this "unseasonable exultation"; he is answered by a confused, honest Englishman. The reasons for the Whig joy on this occasion are found to be their expectation of regaining control of the government, their delight at the prospect of a new war, their hopes of having the Tories hanged, and so on. As for the author of the *Englishman,* Mrs. Manley sarcastically deplores that the sole defense of the Protestant cause should be left to *"Ridpath, Dick Steele,* and their Associates, with the Apostles of *Young Man's* Coffee-House." [61]

Another controversy typical of the war between the *Englishman* and the *Examiner* centered on Robert (later Viscount) Molesworth, a Whig leader in Ireland and a member of the Irish Privy Council.[62] On December 21, the day that the Irish House of Commons petitioned for removal of Sir Constantine Phipps, their Tory Lord Chancellor, Molesworth reportedly made this remark on the defense of Phipps by Convocation: "They that have turned the world upside down, are come hither also." Upon complaints from the Lower House of Convocation to the House of Lords, he was removed from the Privy Council, his remark having been represented as a blasphemous affront to the clergy. Steele, who had earlier praised Molesworth in *Tatler* No. 189, now defended him in *Englishman* No. 46, depicting his removal as a setback to the Constitution.[63] On the other hand, Molesworth was naturally assailed in the Tory press. Swift, in the Dublin edition of *A Preface to the Bishop of Sarum's Introduction,* indicated his feelings by including Molesworth, along with Toland, Tindal, and Collins, in the group of those who, like Burnet, are engaged in attacking all Convocations of the clergy.[64] In the same way he coupled Molesworth and Wharton in a letter to Archbishop King, and he had earlier described him as "the worst of them" in some "Observations" on the Irish Privy Council submitted to Oxford.[65] A month later, in *The Publick Spirit of the Whigs,* he used Steele's defense of Molesworth as evidence of his disrespect for the clergy, calling Steele's position an affront to the "whole Convocation of *Ireland.*" On this issue, then, as on so many in these months, Steele and Swift took rigidly opposed points of view.

In the early months of 1714, the battle between Swift and

Steele over the issue of the Succession entered its major phase. The preliminaries ended with the publication of Steele's *Crisis* on January 19, and from that point on the fight proceeded at a rapid pace. In answer to *The Crisis,* Swift produced *The Publick Spirit of the Whigs,* his most extensive and bitter attack on his old friend. By this time, as we shall see, the Tories were already planning to "punish" Steele for his political writing by expelling him from the House of Commons. Despite his defense of himself in the final paper of the *Englishman* and in his speech before the House, their efforts were successful. Steele lost his seat in Parliament, and his personal quarrel with Swift, by now a public issue, thus reached its climax.

Of all the Whig tracts written in support of the Succession, *The Crisis* is perhaps the most significant. Certainly it is the most pretentious and elaborate. Hanoverian agents assisted in promoting circulation, said to have reached 40,000, and if one may judge by the reaction of Swift and other government writers, the work must have had considerable impact. Steele's main business here is to arouse public opinion to the immediate danger of a Stuart Restoration. To this end, the first and longest section of the tract cites all the laws enacted since the Revolution to defend England against the "Arbitrary Power of a Popish Prince." In his comment on these laws Steele sounds all the usual notes of current Whig propaganda, ranging from a criticism of the Tory peace to an attack on the dismissal of Marlborough; but his principal theme is that the intrigues of the Tories, "our Popish or Jacobite Party," pose an immediate threat to Church and State. Like Burnet, he deplores the indifference of the people in the face of the crisis. Treasonable books striking at the Hanoverian Succession, he complains, are allowed to pass unnoticed. In this connection, Swift, too, is drawn in for attack: "The Author of the Conduct of the Allies has dared to drop Insinuations about altering the Succession." In his effort to stir the public from its lethargy, Steele goes so far as to list Catholic atrocities of the sort to be expected in the event of a Stuart Restoration, and, with rousing rhetoric, he asserts that the only preservation from these "Terrours" is to be found in the laws he has so tediously cited. "It is no time," he writes, "to talk with Hints and Innuendos, but openly and honestly to profess our

Sentiments, before our Enemies have compleated and put their Designs in Execution against us." [66]

Steele apparently professed his sentiments in this book too openly and honestly for his own good, since the government was soon to use it as evidence against him in his trial before the House. In the final issues of the *Englishman,* which ended just as the new session of Parliament began, he provided his enemies with still more ammunition. For example, No. 56 printed the patent giving the Electoral Prince the title of Duke of Cambridge. In a few months the Duke was to be the center of a controversy of some significance on the touchy question of the Protestant Succession. At the order of the Dowager Electress, the Hanoverian agents, supported by the Whig leaders, demanded that a writ of summons be issued which would call the Duke to England to sit in Parliament, thus further insuring the Succession by establishing a Hanoverian Prince in England before the Queen's death. Anne was furious, and Bolingbroke advised that the request be refused. Oxford, realizing that the law required the issuance of the writ, took the opposite view, for which the Queen never forgave him. Accordingly the request was granted, but the Elector himself, who had not been consulted by his mother, rejected the proposal and recalled his agent Schütz, whose impolitic handling of the affair had caused the Hanoverian interest to suffer and had made Oxford's dismissal more likely than ever.[67] Steele in this paper is indicating his sympathy for such a plan. A few days after this *Englishman* appeared, Defoe reported to Oxford that Steele was expected to move in Parliament that the Duke be called over; Defoe then commented, "If they Could Draw that young Gentleman into Their Measures They would show themselves quickly, for they are not asham'd to Say They want Onely a head to Make a beginning." [68]

The final issue of the *Englishman,* No. 57 for February 15, ran to some length and was printed as a separate pamphlet, entitled *The Englishman: Being the Close of the Paper So-called.* Steele's purpose is to present a general defense of his political writing and a résumé of the themes which had occupied him in the *Englishman;* but there is much here also which bears directly on his personal quarrel with Swift. Thus he complains, with considerable justice, that the Tory writers have resorted to libel instead of answering his arguments. His birth, education, and fortune, he says, have all been ridiculed simply because he has spoken with the freedom of an Englishman, and he assures the reader that "whoever talks with me, is speaking to a Gentleman born." [69] As notable examples of this abuse, he quotes passages from the *Examiner*, "that Destroyer of all things," and *The Character of Richard Steele*, which he here attributes to Swift. Though put in rather maudlin terms, Steele's defense of himself has a reasonable basis. His point is simply that the Tories have showered him with personal satire, despite the fact that as a private subject he has a right to speak on political matters without affronting the prerogative of the Sovereign. He claims, too, that his political convictions are simply those which are called "Revolution Principles" and which are accepted by moderate men in both parties.

The final section of this pamphlet is of special interest in a consideration of Steele's relations with Swift. It purports to be a letter from Steele to a friend at court, who, in Miss Blanchard's opinion, could only be meant as Swift. Steele first answers briefly the charges which his "dear old Friend" has made about his pamphlet on Dunkirk and his *Crisis*. Then he launches into an attack on the Tory ministers, whom he calls the "New Converts"; by this term he means to ridicule their professions of acting in the interest of the Church despite their own education and manner of life—a gibe, in other words, at the "Presbyterianism" in Harley's family and at Bolingbroke's reputed impiety. The Tory leaders, he insinuates, are cynically using the Church as a political "By-word" to increase party friction and keep themselves in power. This is the principal point made in this final section of *Englishman* No. 57, and it caps Steele's efforts in his other writing of these months to counteract the notion of the Tories as a "Church Party" supported by the body of the clergy.[70]

Next, Steele turns his attention to the "Courtier" he is addressing. He explains that there are sometimes honorable courtiers, but that too often a man who succeeds at court does not hesitate to sacrifice his Sovereign and nation to his own avarice and ambition. Such, he implies, is the case with his friend, who is not really a new convert himself but merely a favorer of new converts. If "Jack the Courtier" is really to be taken as Swift, the following remark is obviously Steele's comment on Swift's change of parties and its effect on their friendship:

> "I assure you, dear *Jack,* when I first found out such an Allay in you, as makes you of so malleable a Constitution, that you may be worked into any Form an Artificer pleases, I foresaw I should not enjoy your Favour much longer." [71]

He closes his "letter" by demanding that Dunkirk be demolished, that the Pretender be forced to move farther away from the coast of England, and that the Queen and the House of Hanover come to a better understanding. The last point was soon to be included in the "seditious" remarks used against him in Parliament.

The *Examiner,* during Steele's trial a month later, printed an answer from the "courtier" addressed to "R. S." at Button's coffeehouse. He reviews Steele's entrance into politics and finds that his present difficulties are due to his habit of attributing to his own abilities and talents achievements which more properly should be credited to the indulgence of his friends. Once more, in other words, Steele is said to be indebted to Swift for his "wit"; this was the form in which their private feud most often appeared in the Tory press, especially the *Examiner.* In *The Publick Spirit of the Whigs,* it may be noted, Swift himself contemptuously dismissed Steele's reference to his friend at court: "I suppose by the Style of *old Friend,* and the like, it must be some Body *there* of his own Level; among whom, his Party have indeed more *Friends* than I could wish." [72]

On February 16, Steele took his seat in Parliament. By now he was undergoing a fresh torrent of abuse from Tory papers and pamphlets, and action was being taken to effect his punishment by expulsion from Parliament. On the very day that the parliamentary session began, another "Infamous Libel" appeared, entitled *A Letter from the Facetious Dr. Andrew Tripe, at Bath, to the Venerable Nestor Ironside.* It is filled with the usual personal abuse of Steele, especially of his physical appearance; in the opening paragraph, too, Steele is accused of extreme egotism, of giving "himself the preference to all the learned, his contemporaries, from Dr. Sw—ft himself, even down to Poet Cr—spe of the Customhouse." [73] A few days later Defoe wrote Harley that Steele, "The New Champion of The Party," could easily be expelled: "If my Lord The Virulent writeings of this Man May Not be Voted Seditious, None Ever May. . . ." [74] And he set about collecting passages in Steele's writings which could be used as evidence.

In the meantime, before any action was taken in the House, Swift's major attack upon Steele was published. It appeared on February 25, under the title *The Publick Spirit of the Whigs: Set forth in their Generous Encouragement of the Author of the Crisis: with some Observations on the Seasonableness, Candor, Erudition, and Style of that Treatise.* In the history of the duel between Swift and Steele, this is perhaps the most important single document. The bitterness of a personal quarrel of four years' standing and the conflicting political interests and convictions of their recent pamphlet warfare come together here with an intensity not matched by anything else in the story of their relations. One gets the impression that Swift in this answer to *The Crisis* means to finish the fight between them, to silence Steele once and for all; and certainly no reconciliation could be possible after an assault as violent as this one. As the full title indicates, Swift's principal satiric device is to pretend admiration for the generosity of the Whigs, who encourage writers of so little real value to their cause. He professes to envy the liberality with which the "Faction" has treated the triumvirate of leading Whig writers: Dunton, Ridpath, and Steele. The last he characterizes in this way:

> The Third and Principal of this Triumvirate is the Author of the *Crisis;* who, although he must yield to the *Flying-Post* in Knowledge of the World, and Skill in Politicks, and to Mr. *Dunton* in Keenness of Satire, and Variety of Reading; hath yet other Qualities enough to denominate him a Writer of a superior Class to either; provided he would a little regard the Propriety and Disposition of his Words, consult the Grammatical Part, and get some Information in the Subject he intends to handle. [75]

This leads Swift into ridicule of the pretentious advertisements for subscriptions and the *brouhaha* attending the publication of *The Crisis.* The crowning argument for the "implicite Munificence" of Steele's patrons is that his work "was never intended, further than from the Noise, the Bulk, and the Title of *Crisis,* to do any Service to the factious Cause." Not even his title-page, Swift shows, is written with any propriety or common sense.

He then proceeds with a detailed examination of *The Crisis.* Regrettably, the consistently ironic tone of the opening pages is abandoned as he moves through Steele's volume, section by section; his answers to specific points are sometimes matter-of-fact, sometimes brilliantly satiric, sometimes only heavily sarcastic and labored. Steele's dedication to the clergy particularly arouses his ire. By what right, he asks, does Steele direct the clergy what to preach? And how does it happen that the Whigs are now willing for the clergy to concern themselves with politics? They seemed to hold a different view at the time of Sacheverell's trial. And the clergy would never agree with Steele that the Church does not sometimes need the assistance of a secular power, for "upon some Occasions, they want a little *Enlargement of Assistance from the Secular Power,* against *Atheists, Deists, Socinians,* and other Hereticks. . . ." Perhaps Swift is also thinking here of the question of the Sacramental Test, which had played such an important part in his alienation from Steele's party.

Swift, throughout, directs a great deal of personal invective at Steele, ridiculing both his character and his style. He accuses his opponent of putting words together with regard for nothing except cadence, he ridicules Steele's unfortunate description of himself as a "Gentleman born," and he charges him with being a paid incendiary whose arguments are merely the "Spittle of the Bishop of *Sarum.*" As contrasted with *The Importance of the Guardian Considered,* the personal satire here is less amusing, less dependent on irony and indirection; perhaps for that very reason, there emerges slightly more consideration of underlying principles and specific political issues than the design of the earlier pamphlet permitted. Swift attacks, for instance, Steele's discussion in his "Preface" of the doctrines of passive obedience and nonresistance. Not only is that whole matter completely irrelevant to the Succession of the House of Hanover, but Steele's insistent praise of the Revolution is suspicious:

> Are Cases of *extream Necessity* to be produced as common Maxims, by which we are always to proceed? Should not these Gentle-

men sometimes inculcate the general Rule of Obedience, and not always the Exception of Resistance? Since the former hath been the perpetual Dictates of all Laws both Divine and Civil, and the latter is still in Dispute.[76]

In all his political writing Swift consistently viewed the Revolution in just this way, as a case of extreme necessity which did not invalidate the "Rule of Obedience."

As an answer to Steele's main contention, that the Protestant Succession is in danger under the Tory administration, Swift contents himself with outright denial. For him, Steele's propagation of this "artificial Calumny" and "imaginary Danger" is a deliberately inflammatory act designed to arouse the nation against the present government. He comments:

> These are the Opinions which Mr. *Steele* and his Faction, under the Direction of their Leaders, are endeavouring with all their Might to propagate among the People of *England,* concerning the present Ministry; with what Reservation to the Honour, Wisdom, or Justice of the QUEEN, I cannot determine; who by her own free Choice, after long Experience of their Abilities and Integrity, and in Compliance to the general Wishes of her People, called them to her Service. Such an Accusation, against Persons in so high Trust, should require, I think at least, one single Overt-Act to make it good.[77]

Although one cannot take this rhetoric very seriously, it is worth recalling that Swift was, in fact, ignorant of any negotiations between the ministers and the Pretender.

It is worth noting, too, that at one point Swift is given an opportunity to introduce a subject which was very much in his mind just now. Steele had bitterly remarked that the treatment of Marlborough would seem "unaccountable" to posterity. To answer this, Swift gives a brief summary of what an "impartial Historian" will tell future generations, with respect not only to the ambitions of the Duke but also to the conduct of the war, the opposition to the peace, and the encouragement by the Whigs of seditious or irreligious persons and principles. The only aspect of these affairs that posterity will find unaccountable, he says, is that the Duke of Marlborough was dismissed no sooner. Such a summary is not a mere rhetorical device; Swift at this time was seriously concerned that future ages take a correct view of the political events in which he was so closely involved. He himself was actively soliciting for the post of historiographer, and in a memorial to the Queen he stressed the danger of future misrepresentation of such matters as the change of ministries in 1710, the peace negotiations, or the fall of Marlborough. "It is necessary," he wrote, "for the honour of the Queen and in justice to her servants, that some able hand should be immediately employed to write the history of her Majesty's reign; that the truth of things may be transmitted to future ages, and bear down the falsehood of malicious pens." [78] Despite the fact that his efforts to obtain the official post were unsuccessful, he was later to serve as this "able hand" in such works as his *Memoirs* and the *Enquiry*. The author of *The Crisis,* himself one of these "malicious pens," had struck in an area where Swift was particularly sensitive.

To Steele's charge that Jacobite books were being disseminated without government action, Swift replies with a simple *tu quoque.* It is just as great an evil, he says, "to see seditious Books *dispersed among us, apparently striking at the QUEEN* and her Administration, at the Constitution in Church and State, and at all Religion. . . ." In a sense, this is the gist of his whole reply to Steele's pamphlet. In his view, the Succession was in no danger, and Steele's expressions of alarm were only an excuse for insolent, seditious attacks upon the government. By Steele's own admission, Swift points out, the Succession is established and confirmed by several laws. These statutes are certainly better securities against a Stuart Restoration than those which the Whigs would substitute in their place, such as "a Report of the QUEEN's Death; an *Effigies* of the *Pretender* run twice through the Body by a valiant Peer: A Speech by the Author of the *Crisis:* And to sum up all, an unlimited Freedom of reviling her Majesty, and those she employs." [79]

If nothing else, *The Publick Spirit of the Whigs* demonstrates once more that Steele was no match for Swift and the other Tory writers. Beside this fiercely satiric pamphlet, *The Crisis* seems pale and ineffectual indeed. Nor could Swift's victory in this pamphlet war be endangered by such clumsy invective as *The Publick Spirit of the Tories, Manifested in the Case of the Irish Dean and his Man Timothy,* probably by Steele's friend

Thomas Burnet. In a few weeks, however, he must have regretted a section of his work which reflected on the Scottish peers and on the Union between England and "a poor, fierce Northern People." On March 2, his tract was condemned, and the Queen, when petitioned to do so by the House, issued a proclamation offering a reward of £300 for discovery of the author. It was common knowledge that the book was the work of Swift, who, in one observer's opinion, "hath more wit then judgment." He was successfully shielded, however, and the matter was dropped with the prosecution of the printer by the Earl of Mar. Swift was resentful, feeling that he had been made to suffer for writing in support of the government; yet, as Professor Davis points out, it is puzzling that the ministers should have allowed him to include an attack on the Scottish nobility when they depended on that group for their majority in Lords.[80]

At the same time, Steele, too, was suffering as a result of his political writing. On March 10, Defoe sent an analysis of "seditious" passages in Steele's writings to Oxford. Two days later Thomas Foley, a relative of Harley's, made the complaint in the House, and the debate was held on March 18. When the vote was taken, even the "Whimsicals" sided with the government, and Steele was expelled from Commons. The "punishment" which the Tories had contemplated for many months had now been administered.

The proceedings of the trial and Steele's three-hour speech of defense were later printed in his *Apology*, not published until well after the death of the Queen. The speech itself deserves some comment. Very clearly, the basic issue was his right as a private subject to attack the policies of the ministry. Opposition to Oxford and Bolingbroke, he felt, could hardly be equated with opposition to the Queen. It was the same position he had taken in the Dunkirk controversy, when the Tories had charged him with a treasonable affront to the royal prerogative. Yet his speech before Commons carefully avoids this line of argument. Instead, he sets out to show that the passages cited against him, from *The Crisis* and *Englishman* Nos. 46 and 57, are completely innocent, devoid even of any reflections upon the ministers. He asserts, for example, that his expressions of alarm for the security of the Succession are to be applied naturally to avowed

Jacobites and "Popish Emissaries," not to Oxford and Bolingbroke. Only at the end of his speech does he declare his right
to criticize the administration freely and legally. It is the duty
of Commons, he concludes, to protect their members from the
"Resentments of any single Minister." There can be little doubt
that the restraint of his speech, which contrasts markedly with
the comments which accompany it in the *Apology*, was due to
the influence of Addison. Steele acknowledges that much of his
speech was written by friends, whose discretion prevented him
from adding to his arguments "many honest Truths." According
to Smithers, Addison sat beside Steele, prompting from notes,
and after the speech was over he followed his friend out of the
House to restrain him from any rash action.[81]

One major aspect of Steele's speech directly involved Swift.
He opened his defense with an impassioned attack on the
Examiner. All of his pamphlets which are cited as objectionable,
says Steele, were written as answers to this Tory journalist who
has given himself the air of being in the secrets of the ministry
and has attacked him with "groundless Calumnies." He continues: "Such has been the cruel and ungenerous Usage which
I have met with from an Author who has several times professed
himself a Champion for the Ministry, that no longer since than
last *Friday* he has fallen upon me with that Rage and Malice,
which is unbecoming a Scholar, a Gentleman, or a Christian. . . ."[82] He enumerates at length the offenses of this unnamed writer, which include vilifying Britain's Allies, condemn-
ing treaties still in force, and destroying the reputation of the
most eminent persons. All of this has been done not only with
impunity but with encouragement from those in high station.
In short, Steele says, this entire affair now laid before the House
of Commons is no more than a "Paper War between two private
Persons." Then, after this long attack on the *Examiner,* Steele
suddenly seizes upon an opportunity to mention Swift by name
and to reflect bitterly on the change in their relationship. As
proof of his respect for the clergy and the Church, he cites several passages from his works, and among them he quotes the
paragraph in *Tatler* No. 5 praising the author of *A Project for
the Advancement of Religion.* He then comments:

> The Gentleman I here intended was Dr. *Swift;* this kind of Man
> I thought him at that time: We have not met of late, but I hope
> he deserves this Character still.[83]

The citation of this passage from the *Tatler* is curiously ironic,
perhaps deliberately so, in view of the fact that only a few weeks
earlier Swift himself, in *The Publick Spirit of the Whigs,* had
charged that Steele was disrespectful to the clergy and had offered unspecified essays in the *Tatler* as evidence. For some in
Steele's audience, too, his comment on the passage must have
had a certain dramatic value. Here, before a House of Commons
assembled to adjudge his fitness to sit as one of their members,
Steele summarizes with one terse sarcasm the history of his estrangement from Swift. His earlier remarks had left no doubt
that he considered the Dean at least partly responsible for his
present predicament. Since the publication of *Guardian* No. 53,
their private quarrel had become more and more a subject for
public comment and partisan exploitation. Steele's reference to
Swift in his speech of defense represents the culmination of that
trend, and, in a sense, the climax of three and a half years of
increasing bitterness between the two men whose friendship
could not withstand the press of political conflict.

4.

Steele's reputation had suffered greatly as a result of his political activity. The account of his expulsion given by the Tory
Thomas Hearne is an interesting reflection of ministerial propaganda. Hearne writes:

> He was a rakish, wild, drunken Spark; but he got a good Reputa-
> tion by publishing a Paper that came out daily called the Tattler,
> and by another called the Spectator; but the most ingenious of
> these Papers were written by Mr Addison, and Dr Swift, as 'tis
> reported. And when these two had left him, he appeared to be
> a mean, heavy weak Writer as is sufficiently demonstrated in his
> Papers called the Guardian, the Englishman, and the Lover. He
> now writes for Bread, being involved in Debt.[84]

That Steele's "wit" was really only the contributions of his
friends had been one of the major themes of Swift, the *Examiner,*

and the other personal attacks directed against him. Aitken mentions, for example, a poem of this period in which Swift is chided for his treatment of Steele and is made to admit, "I boast my Art's success; whate'er he writ / Is nonsense now, if his; and mine if wit." [85] Nor is it surprising that Hearne should speak in such favorable terms of Addison. Throughout this period of turbulent party warfare, Addison was content to remain in the background, quietly supervising Whig propagandists and maneuvering to preserve Whig literary prestige. He was not attacked by the Tory journalists, and on the one occasion when he did contribute to the propaganda campaign against the terms of the peace (*The Trial of Count Tariff*), his name was apparently not even connected with the pamphlet. Consequently, his stature in literary circles remained unimpaired, respected by both parties. Unlike "poor Dick," he was too cautious to permit his "zeal for the public" to be "ruinous to himself."

After his expulsion from Commons, Steele continued to write, probably "for Bread," in Hearne's phrase, but certainly for the political cause to which he had dedicated himself. He had again turned to periodical essays in the *Lover,* which ran for forty numbers, from February 25 to May 27. For the most part this journal is nonpolitical, but just after the proceedings against Steele in the House, a number of issues are devoted to satirizing the Harleys—especially Oxford and Foley—as the "Crabtree Family." In No. 16 (April 1), Steele includes in his ridicule of the Crabtrees an attack on Swift by the timeworn method of criticizing *A Tale of a Tub.* Sir Anthony (Oxford) is said to take his politics from Swift's book, which Steele first calls a "Book of Humour and Ridicule" and then a work "written for the advancement of Religion only." Oxford's manner of conducting levees, Steele writes, is derived from Lord Peter's whispering-office. A few lines from Swift describing that invention are broken off with the comment, "The other Parts of that Paragraph are too course to be repeated." [86] After a few more essays satirizing the "execrable race of the Crabtrees," Steele excluded politics from the *Lover.* Instead, he made an effort to publish simultaneously with the *Lover* a completely partisan journal called the *Reader;* this venture, however, came to an end on May 10, after only nine issues. The themes of this uninspired paper are nothing new: Dunkirk, the Succession, the new converts, the Duke of Cambridge writ, and so on. Most of all, though, Steele concerns himself with answering the *Examiner*. No allusion is made to Swift's hand in the Tory paper, although the anonymity of its author comes in for attack:

> I therefore . . . pronounce all the Nonsense which the *Examiner* ever has, or ever shall utter, . . . to be of no Effect, or of any Moment with regard to Life, Limb, Honour, or Fame of any of Her Majesty's Subjects, because no one knows who he is; and I pronounce the same of the *Post-Boy*, because every body knows who he is.[87]

Steele's other political writing in the spring of 1714 need not concern us. There are no allusions to Swift in his final pamphlets in the reign of Anne, except insofar as his readers would have equated the Dean and the *Examiner*. But by this time there were others quite ready to state Steele's case against Swift. In May there appeared an anonymous volume entitled *Essays Divine, Moral and Political: By the Author of the Tale of a Tub, sometime the Writer of the Examiner, and the Original Inventor of the Band-Box-Plot*. One of its major themes is Swift's *"Breach of Friendship"* with Steele, whom he has pursued *"with a Violence inconsistent with the Character of a Friend, and unworthy of that of a* Clergyman *and* Christian." [88] The motto on the title page is "Out of thy own Mouth will I condemn Thee, O thou Hypocrite," and much of the book does, in fact, consist of shreds and patches of various works by Swift, taken out of context and turned against him. Underlying this entire attack, as I have noted previously, is the effort to place Swift in an egoistic school of moralists; for the *persona* in this satire, self-love is the root of all behavior, and the design of the book is for "Swift" to explain how this principle has operated for him in various fields of endeavor. In the "Dedication to Prince Posterity," he is said to have three characters: as a critic, he ridicules religion; as the *Examiner*, he abuses his old friends; and as a clergyman, he writes projects for the reformation of manners. It was with much the same ironic intention, of course, that Steele had invoked Swift's *Project* in his speech of defense before the House of Commons. Next, "Swift" justifies himself from two alleged crimes. One is that he has libelled Wharton and the Junto, who were once his friends and benefactors; this is answered easily enough: *"The* Times, *the* Ministry *are chang'd, and why should not I?"* The other charge involves his treatment of Steele, which again is justified by his guiding principle:

> As for Friendship, when it interferes with Interest, its a Shadow, a Nothing: . . . Now my Interest was manifestly in Danger, for he had disoblig'd my most Noble Patron, and I was judg'd the fittest Person to revenge his Injuries, since, by my Intimacy with Dick, I had found the Way into his Bosom, and knew his Weak Side. I undertook the Work, and glory in the Performance. . . .[89]

The "Work" referred to is *The Character of Richard Steele;* Swift's supposed authorship of that tract is the principal accusation of those sections of the *Essays* dealing with Steele.

The essays themselves are similar in tone to the Dedication. The first, using appropriate passages from *A Tale of a Tub,* shows the origin of religion to be vapors. The second, "Of Christianity," uses Swift's *Argument against the Abolishing of Christianity* against him by repeating its arguments without its irony, and so on. It is in the fifth essay, "Of Friendship," that Swift's relationship with Steele is most fully discussed. As usual, it begins with a statement of general principle: in reality, there is no such thing as friendship, since *self* is involved and, as always, is paramount. What passes for friendship, in any rank of society, is merely self-interest. Nevertheless, the appearance of friendship can be a valuable tool on occasion, such as undermining the reputation of rivals in fame:

> After this manner, I acted with Mr. *Steele* . . . . And tho' at last he has discover'd me to be his *Enemy,* yet I led him into so many Steps of Ruin, whilst he was my *Friend,* that it's now impossible for him to extricate himself. My *Reputation* now rises superiour to his, and is quite of a different Nature; so that the Name of *Friend* is of no further Use, and I can trample on him, with a better Grace, as a Declar'd Enemy.[90]

Thus, "Swift's" barbarous treatment of Steele is the result of envy of his literary reputation. To demonstrate the manner in which he proceeded, he summarizes his relations with Steele from the days of the *Tatler* to his open assault upon his friend in *The Character of Richard Steele.* According to this account,

Swift was at first quite willing to help Steele with the *Tatler,* primarily because all the celebrated wits were engaged in the enterprise and he was unwilling to be left out. So he contributed a name, Bickerstaff, and a few pieces. But he soon realized that his friend's reputation was growing too great, and he secretly plotted Steele's undoing. The method, he saw, was easy; the way to ruin Steele was to lead him into party warfare. Consequently, he advised him to print the letter from Downes the prompter (the satire on Harley in *Tatler* No. 193), which was the beginning of Steele's decline. He "sour'd all his *Tory* Readers" with that essay, and they began ascribing all the witty papers to Swift (this, in effect, is only a slight distortion of what actually happened). Then "Swift" gradually withdrew his assistance, after first attempting to persuade Steele to write a recantation, which would have ruined him with both parties. He concludes: "But, at length, tir'd with Acting a double Character, I threw off the Mask, and appear'd a Confess'd Enemy, attack'd him openly, under the Character of *Toby.* . . ." Thus, he says, do all friendships end.

The authorship of this curious attack on Swift must remain a matter of conjecture. It is customarily attributed to Thomas Burnet, Steele's friend and the son of Bishop Burnet, but Professor D. Nichol Smith has pointed out the lack of evidence for this attribution. In the nineteenth century, Dilke and Craik both agreed that Steele himself was the writer of these *Essays.*[91] According to their reasoning, no one but Steele would have thought it worth while to comment at such length on his personal relations with Swift. Yet there is no circumstance in this account of their quarrel which would not have been known to anyone well acquainted with the political journalism of the period. And by this time, as we have seen, their personal differences had become a common enough motif in political satire directed at either of them. Though it is possible that this was the work of someone close to Steele, it need not have been so. It remains, at any rate, as evidence of the complete disintegration of a friendship.

Swift took no notice of this attack. By now he was thoroughly disgusted with politics, especially with the dissensions among the Tories themselves. "Our situation is so bad," he wrote, "that our enemies could not, without abundance of invention and ability, have placed us so ill, if we had left it entirely to their management." [92] In this mood, he left London on June 1 for the rectory of Letcombe Basset in Berkshire. From this vantage point he was able to write an incisive analysis of the present state of affairs, so dangerous to him and his party. He was to remain in retirement until after the death of the Queen on August 1, the event which meant complete defeat for him and victory for Addison and Steele.

Swift's withdrawal from the political scene caused consternation among his friends and amusement among his enemies. Pope wrote to him:

> At Button's it is reported you are gone to Hanover, and that Gay goes only on an embassy to you. Others apprehend some dangerous state treatise from your retirement, and a wit who affects to imitate Balzac, says, that the Ministry now are like those heathens of old who received their oracles from the woods.[93]

While his friends kept him informed of the latest phase of the struggle between Oxford and Bolingbroke, Swift was writing a dispassionate commentary on the current situation. *Some Free Thoughts upon the Present State of Affairs* was finished July 1 and sent by Ford to a printer, who forwarded the manuscript to Bolingbroke for revision. Bolingbroke kept the copy until after the Queen's death. His delay is not difficult to understand, for Swift has not hesitated in this essay to blame both the ambitious Bolingbroke and the dilatory Oxford for the crisis at Court. The struggle between the two ministers he compares to "a Ship's Crew quarrelling in a Storm, or while their Enemies are within Gun Shott."

But Swift's criticism in this discourse is not entirely negative. He emphasizes that two major steps must be taken, both of which are in accord with the wishes of the nation. The first involves strengthening the "Church interest":

> First, that the Church of England should be preserved entire in all Her Rights, Powers and Priviledges; All Doctrines relating to Government discouraged which She condemns; All Schisms, Sects and Heresies discountenanced and kept under due Subjection, as far as consists with the Lenity of our Constitution. Her open

Enemies (among whom I include at least Dissenters of all Denominations) not trusted with the smallest Degree of Civil or
Military Power; and Her secret Adversaries under the Names of
Whigs, Low-Church, Republicans, Moderation-Men, and the like,
receive no Marks of Favour from the Crown, but what they
should deserve by a sincere Reformation.[94]

To a contemporary, I think, this would have sounded like unqualified approval of Bolingbroke's Schism Bill, which Steele
had attacked and on which Swift never commented directly. In
essence, the passage is a statement of Swift's faith in the role of
the Tories as a "Church party" and of his consistently rigorous
attitude toward political toleration of the sects: the desirability
of the Sacramental Test is clearly suggested. Here, then, as this
brilliant phase of Swift's life was drawing to a close, he reasserts
that loyalty to his Church which had been of fundamental importance in his disillusionment with the Whigs in 1710.

The second point which Swift emphasizes is the security of
the Protestant Succession. Here he is interested less in making
specific proposals than in dispelling the fears of those who believe
that the ministers are engaged in Jacobite intrigue. Once again
he states, with complete assurance, that the Hanoverian Succession is "as firmly secured as the Nature of the Thing can
possibly admit," by the oaths of abjuration, by the nature of
High Church principles, by the inclination of the people and the
insignificance of the Pretender. More important, he answers the
objections of those like Steele who see danger to the Succession
in the "Tory" principles of passive obedience, nonresistance, and
hereditary right. The highest Tories, says Swift, look upon the
Revolution as a part of history. They feel that "the Inheritance
to the Crown is in pursuance of Laws made ever since their
Remembrance, by which all Papists are excluded; and they have
no other Rule to go by." The doctrines of passive obedience
and hereditary right they find necessary for preserving the present Establishment and for continuing the Succession in the House
of Hanover. Though Swift will not try to justify this creed in
all its parts, yet, he says, "I am sure it sets the Protestant Succession upon a much firmer Foundation, than all the indigested
Scheams of those who profess to act upon what they call Revo-
lution-Principles." [95]

Nevertheless, the Whigs have prevailed upon the Elector to ask for some further security, and Swift considers the problem of satisfying him without endangering the honor or safety of the Queen. His suggestion is that the eldest grandson of the Elector be invited over; the presence of that infant Prince could not be inconsistent with the Queen's safety, since he could not be corrupted in his principles or exposed to vicious influences. One of Swift's reasons for making this proposal is that it enables him to condemn by contrast the Whig agitation over the Duke of Cambridge writ and the collaboration between Hanoverian agents and Whig leaders. He writes:

> But, as all this is most manifestly unnecessary in it self, and only in Complyance with the mistaken Doubts of a presumptive Heir; so the Nation would (to speak in the Language of Mr. Steele) *Expect* that her Majesty should be made perfectly easy from that Side for the future; No more be alarmed with Apprehensions of Visits or Demands of Writs, where She hath not thought fit to give any Invitation.[96]

Swift concludes his *Free Thoughts* with a reassertion of his central point: the only way of securing the Constitution and the Protestant Succession (and, of course, the Tory administration) is to lessen the power of domestic enemies as much as possible. If this is not done, the ministers will be able to blame only themselves for the triumph of their adversaries.

The moving force behind this essay was Swift's fear that the Tories, unless serious steps were taken, would be faced with a complete loss of power on the death of the Queen. Writing to the Earl of Peterborough in May, he had complained that everyone at Court acted as if the Queen were immortal. "Neither is it possible," he wrote, "to persuade people to make any preparations against an evil day." [97] But the evil day came, even before the *Free Thoughts* could be published. On July 27, Oxford was finally dismissed. Bolingbroke, however, had little opportunity to consolidate his new position; two days later Queen Anne fell ill, and on August 1, Swift received the news that she was dead.

The government of England was now in the hands of a Board of Regents or "Lords Justices," comprising seven officers of state and eighteen others appointed by the King. Bolingbroke was not among them. The great question now for Swift and his friends was the extent to which the accession of George I would mean a political triumph for the Whigs. Bolingbroke, writing to Swift, seemed sanguine enough:

> What a world is this, and how does Fortune banter us. . . .
> The Tories seem to resolve not to be crushed; and that is enough
> to prevent them from being so. . . . I have lost all by the death
> of the Queen, but my spirit; and I protest to you, I feel that in-
> crease upon me.[98]

Swift's friend, Charles Ford, also expected few changes. But Swift was more realistic than either. To Bolingbroke he replied, "Thus your machine of four years modelling is dashed to pieces in a moment; and, as well by the choice of the Regents as by their proceedings, I do not find there is any intention of managing you in the least." In much the same vein he wrote to Ford: "I think the Regents agree pretty well in their Choice of Persons, and that we are this moment under the Height of a Whig Administration. You do not mention Addison; who M^r L says is Secretary to the Regency." [99]

Addison had, in fact, been chosen unanimously as the Secretary to the group of Regents whom Swift described as "the rankest Whigs, except 4 or 5 Proselytes, which is worse . . . ." Addison's new post, for which he had been proposed by Halifax, was a significant administrative position, so important that it was rumored he would be made a Secretary of State when the King arrived. For Steele, too, the Queen's death was good news. On August 4, he wrote to his wife, "I have been loaded with Compliments from the Regents and assured of something immediately. . . ." [100] Thus, the collapse of the political cause to which Swift had dedicated himself for four years could bring only good fortune to his former friends Addison and Steele. The complete reversal of their positions emerges, too, in the juxtaposition of two bits of Peter Wentworth's gossip:

> Mr. Addison being made secretary to the Lords justice makes
> people fancy he'll be one of the secretarys of State when the
> King comes, and the report runs that he had orders to settle
> all Lord Bullingbrook's papers, but there's nothing of that. . . .
> This day there's a very cleaver banter come out upon doctor Swift,
> wch if you stay I must send you.[101]

The "banter" may have been Jonathan Smedley's *An Hue and Cry after Dr. S—t,* a satire in the form of Swift's "diary" during a week of his seclusion before the Queen's death. It contains several scattered references to Swift's break with Addison and Steele, such as "Resolv'd to write to *D. S—le,*" "By G—d *Steele* has got the better of me," or *"Ad—n* says I am gone to hang my self." It was typical of the many attacks on Swift which resulted from the fall of the Tory ministry. A month later he remarked, "I shall be cured of loving England, as the fellow was of his ague, by getting himself whipped through the town." [102]

On August 16, Swift left for Ireland to take the oaths of allegiance in the new reign. He had offered his services to Bolingbroke and expressed his willingness to return in the winter, but he realized well enough that this "new world," unlike that of 1710, had no place for him. He was not to return to England for almost twelve years. Since 1708, the paths of Swift, Addison, and Steele had so diverged, that what was now for them an occasion for joy could only fill him with the deepest pessimism. The return to power of their party meant his separation from his friends and the defeat of those interests which he sincerely believed to be essential to the security of his Church and State. Just before his departure, Arbuthnot drew a moral from the present situation with which Swift could only have agreed: "I have an opportunity calmly and philosophically to consider that treasure of vileness and baseness, that I always believed to be in the heart of man. . . ." [103]

5.

Swift's departure for Ireland meant separation not only from his close friends in the Tory Scriblerus Club but from those among the Whig wits with whom he had once been intimate. Consequently, his later relations with Addison and Steele may be sketched fairly briefly. The bitter quarrel with Steele had left too deep an impression for their friendship to be renewed, even at a distance. Addison, however, he had never ceased to respect, and it was not difficult for these two men to reassert their mutual admiration and esteem, now that the pressure of immediate political conflict had been relieved. But they never saw each other again, for Addison died before Swift was able to return to England.

Under the new Whig administration, both Steele and Addison were rewarded for their political constancy. Steele received gifts of money, knighthood, and the governorship of the Drury Lane Theater. He was also once more a member of Parliament. Addison, with reasons for greater expectations, was at first less successful. Instead of the appointment as Secretary of State which he had expected, he was made Chief Secretary to the Earl of Sunderland, the new Lord Lieutenant of Ireland—the same office which he had held in 1708. Because of Sunderland's illness, however, neither he nor his Secretary ever went to Ireland, so that Addison and Swift were not able to resume the intimacy which they had enjoyed during Addison's previous tenure of that office. When the Lord Lieutenant resigned in 1715, Addison was again without employment, except for his seat in Commons. Towards the end of that year he was made a Commissioner of Trades and Plantations, and in 1717, finally, he became Secretary of State.

The Whig supremacy under which Addison and Steele now flourished produced exasperating difficulties for Dean Swift. In the fall of 1714, for example, he found himself opposed by Archbishop King, with whom his relationship had gradually deteriorated because of political differences. King wished to appoint only Whig clergymen to vacant benefices. At this time, he and Swift had different candidates for the chancellorship of the cathedral and the benefice of St. Nicholas Without; and King wrote urging the appointment of his reliable Whigs not only to Sunderland but to his Secretary Addison, a friend who had first been recommended to him by Swift himself.[104]

If Swift was aware of Addison's involvement in his quarrels with King, he gave no sign of it. In October he was writing *Memoirs relating to that Change which happened in the Queen's Ministry,* where Addison is referred to as his "old and intimate acquaintance." These *Memoirs* are primarily a personal *apologia,* a justification of his role as Tory journalist and an explanation of the consistency of his political principles. By coincidence, Steele in the same month also wrote his *Apology,* the defense of his political career which centers on his expulsion from Parliament. Here he prints in full his speech of defense, with its attack on Swift. The dedication to Walpole and the remarks accompanying the speech bitterly indict the *Examiner* and the Earl of Oxford.

In 1715, matters took a serious turn for Swift and his Tory friends. A Committee of Secrecy was appointed to gather materials for the impeachment of the ministers and others, like Prior, who had been involved in the peace negotiations. Bolingbroke fled to France, where, in the summer, he was followed by Ormond; Oxford remained to stand trial. Those who had attacked the "Jacobitism" of the previous ministry now felt that their suspicions were justified. Addison, in his letters, reported the proceedings of the Committee in a satisfied tone, although he resolved to be absent "as by accident" on the day the vote was taken to impeach Ormond, who had befriended him as Chancellor of Oxford and Lord Lieutenant of Ireland. Swift, on the other hand, was naturally quite alarmed. In June he wrote to Pope:

> You know how well I loved both Lord Oxford and Bolingbroke, and how dear the Duke of Ormond is to me. Do you imagine I can be easy while their enemies are endeavouring to take off their heads. . . . Do you imagine I can be easy, when I think of the probable consequences of these proceedings, perhaps upon the very peace of the nation, but certainly of the minds of so many hundred thousand good subjects? [105]

Swift had good reason to be uneasy. Just a month before, two packets sent to him by the Duchess of Ormond's chaplain had been intercepted in Dublin; they contained "seditious" pamphlets and letters from the Duke of Ormond and John Barber. This material was transmitted to Archbishop King and the Earl of Kildare, then acting Lords Justices, who in turn sent the letters to Stanhope, Secretary of State. Addison's kinsman Eustace Budgell also sent copies to Sunderland. The Lord Lieutenant, through his private secretary, acknowledged King's "zeal and diligence" and expressed the hope that "if there appears enough against the Doctor to justify it he is kept in confinement. . . ." Swift, however, had not answered letters of this sort, and no effort was made to prosecute him.[106] Addison, actually in charge of Irish affairs while Sunderland was at Bath, must have known of his friend's predicament, but he makes no reference to it. Nor was the incident mentioned to him by King, although the Archbishop sent him four letters during this month.

Distressed at the persistence with which the Whigs were seeking their revenge, and shocked especially by the attainder of the Duke of Ormond (June 21, 1715), Swift at once began composition of *An Enquiry into the Behaviour of the Queen's Last Ministry*. For five years he worked intermittently at this defense of his friends, which was not printed until after his death. "As my own Heart was free from all treasonable Thoughts," he writes, "so I did little Imagine my self to be perpetually in the Company of Traytors. But *the Fashion of this World passeth away*." [107] Steele, meanwhile, was engaged in an undertaking of just the opposite sort. One of the primary objectives of the second series of his *Englishman,* which ran from July 11 to November 21, was the justification of the impeachment proceedings. Bolingbroke and Oxford are viciously attacked as Jacobites who negotiated a peace favoring France. Steele makes no allusion to Swift in these papers, but once again political and personal loyalties had led them to take contrasting positions.

The Jacobite rebellion in the fall of 1715 made papers such as Steele's more necessary than ever, and in December Addison began the *Freeholder,* a periodical designed to secure popular opinion in favor of the Whig administration. He had lost his employment as Irish Secretary in the summer, and for a time contemplated a trip to Ireland to take the oaths as Keeper of the Records, the Irish office which he had held even during the Tory ministry. By way of St. George Ashe, he sent friendly messages to Swift; but he later decided against making this visit.[108] On December 20, he finally secured membership in the Board of Trade, and a few days later the first issue of the *Freeholder* appeared. Addison's themes here are not surprising. He praises and defends Whig principles in general and specific acts of the ministry in dealing with the rebellion, such as the suspension of habeas corpus. He insists that Toryism means Jacobitism and draws a sharply satiric sketch of a Tory fox hunter, which contrasts with the *Spectator*'s more subtle ridicule of Sir Roger de Coverly. Many of his papers are panegyrics on the King, whose popularity was rapidly waning. As one would expect, Addison's tone in this paper, which continued until June 29, 1716, is consistently urbane, with no lapses into personal abuse or bitter recriminations.

It is curious that as late as 1727 Swift should have taken the trouble to annotate passages in the *Freeholder,* yet this is what seems to have happened. The majority of his notes are merely sarcastic comments on Addison's defense of the King and the "lenity" of the Whig government. Swift is concerned, as usual, to defend Oxford and his associates from the charge of Jacobitism. Addison, for example, reflects upon Ormond, who had joined the Pretender, and Swift answers, "Driven out by tyranny, malice, and faction." Or, again, *Freeholder* No. 2 speaks of the interposition of Providence in removing obstacles to the King's succession, "in taking away, at so critical a juncture, the person who might have proved a dangerous enemy. . . ." The "person" meant, of course, is Oxford, but Swift retorts, "False, groundless, invidious, and ungrateful. Was that person the Queen?" Swift, in general, makes very few remarks about Addison himself. At one point, though, the *Freeholder* suggests that one should occasionally sacrifice doubts so as to concur with the judgment of ministerial leaders; for Swift, this is a "motion to make men go every length with their party." And he adds, "I am sorry to see such a principle in this author." It may be noted, finally, that Swift passes over without comment *Freeholder* No. 19 (February 24, 1715/16), in which Addison attacks in retrospect the Tory *Examiner* and asserts that it was written "by those among them whom they looked upon as their most celebrated wits and politicians. . . ." [109]

On July 9, 1717, Swift wrote to the Earl of Oxford, congratulating him on his acquittal and offering to accompany him into retirement. Perhaps the pleasure he felt at the outcome of Oxford's trial also moved him to think at this time of his friend Addison, who had recently been appointed Secretary of State. At any rate, on the same day he sent a letter of congratulations to the new Secretary, his first direct correspondence with Addison since the fall of the Tories. He thanks Addison for the overtures he had made through Bishop Ashe when planning a visit to Ireland, and he acknowledges the Secretary's willingness to make "party give way to friendship." Addison's appointment, writes Swift, has given an easy mind to many people, "who will never believe any ill can be intended to the Constitution in Church and State, while you are in so high a trust. . . ." He continues:

> I examine my heart, and can find no other reason why I write to you now, beside that great love and esteem I have always had for you. I have nothing to ask you either for any friend or for myself. When I conversed among Ministers, I boasted of your acquaintance, but I feel no vanity from being known to a Secretary of State. I am only a little concerned to see you stand single; for it is a prodigious singularity in any Court to owe one's rise entirely to merit.[110]

A few more such appointments, Swift concludes, would gain more converts for the Whigs in three weeks "than all the methods hitherto practised have been able to do in as many years."

Addison apparently was able to answer this letter only in March of the following year, by which time he had resigned from the Secretary's office after a protracted illness. Swift must have written at least one other letter before this, for the terms of Addison's reply make it clear that the Dean had requested political favors for some unnamed friend. He reports that Swift's letter containing this request has been turned over to James Craggs, his successor as Secretary. "I know," he writes, "you have so much zeal and pleasure in doing kind offices for those you wish well to, that I hope you represent the hardship of the case in the strongest colours that it can possibly bear." [111] He expresses his sorrow at the death of their mutual friend, Bishop Ashe. "Shall we never again talk together in laconic?" Addison asks, and he concludes by inviting Swift to Holland House, his new residence since his marriage to the Countess of Warwick in 1716.

On October 1, 1718, Addison again answered a letter from Swift which has not been preserved. Apparently it also concerned the friend for whom Swift had requested his aid, for Addison promises to negotiate further in the matter, in which Bishop Ashe's family was evidently interested as well as Swift. He then expresses his hope once more of seeing Swift in England, and he reports having talked of Swift with Smalridge, Bishop of Bristol: "We have often talked of you, and when I assure you he has an exquisite taste of writing, I need not tell you how he

talks on such a subject." Addison then indicates his pleasure
that no consideration of party differences is able now to endanger
their friendship:

> I look upon it as my good fortune, that I can express my esteem
> of you, even to those who are not of the Bishop's party, without
> giving offence. When a man has so much compass in his character,
> he affords his friends topics enough to enlarge upon, that all sides
> admire.[112]

This was Swift's last exchange of correspondence with Addison,
and it is ironic that here at the end of their relationship we
find Swift soliciting favors from Addison, now a man of prestige
and considerable power in the nation's dominant political group.
Only a few years earlier the situation had been exactly the
reverse.

On June 17, 1719, Addison died. Only a few months earlier
he had split with Steele over the Peerage Bill, with Addison's
Old Whig opposing Steele's series, the *Plebian*. His relations
with Steele had deteriorated since about 1717. As Mr. Smithers
observes, their estrangement forms an interesting contrast with
the fact that the friendship between Addison and Swift had
somehow managed to survive, despite totally different political
convictions.[113] Swift was proud of the manner in which he and
Addison had overcome the political bitterness which had in-
fected their friendship in the last years of Queen Anne. In 1725,
he wrote to Addison's friend and biographer Tickell, "None but
converts are afraid of showing favour to those who lie under
suspicion in point of principles; and that was Mr. Addison's
argument, in openly continuing his friendship to me to the very
hour of his death." And in 1729 he included Addison in his list
of friends "famous for their learning, wit, or great employments
or quality." [114]

Steele's name was not included in this list. Swift never forgave
him for his "continually repeated indiscretions, and a zeal
mingled with scurrilities," as the Dean phrased it well after
Steele's death in 1729.[115] There had been too much bitterness on
both sides for any possibility of a reconciliation, and Swift seldom named Steele in his letters or writings after 1714. It is worth
noting, though, that both Addison and Steele are used as satiric

exempla in *A Libel on D— D— and a Certain Great Lord,* written in 1730 to ridicule Delany's efforts to gain preferment by
praising Lord Carteret in verse. To demonstrate the ingratitude
of great lords to men of wit, Swift gives the examples of Congreve, Steele, Gay, and Addison. Of the last he writes:

> Thus *Addison* by Lords Carest,
> Was left in Foreign Lands distrest,
> Forgot at Home, became for Hire,
> A trav'lling Tutor to a *Squire;*
> But, wisely left the *Muses* Hill,
> To Bus'ness shap'd the *Poet's* Quil,
> Let all his barren Lawrel's fade
> Took up himself the *Courtier's* Trade,
> And grown a *Minister of State,*
> Saw Poets at his Levee wait.

Swift is slightly ironic, of course, in his description of Addison's
substitution of a political for a poetic career, and later in the
poem he parodies a simile from the *Campaign.* But on the whole
the lines are not too severe, especially in the context of this bitter
satire. Much harsher is his account of Steele:

> Thus, *Steel* who own'd what others writ,
> And flourish'd by imputed Wit,
> From Lodging in a hundred Jayls,
> Was left to starve, and dye in *Wales.*[116]

This sketch is too abusive, really, to make perfect sense as an
exemplum of the mistreatment of literary men by those whom
they seek to flatter. As Williams's note points out, Steele's later
difficulties—highly exaggerated by Swift—resulted from his own
improvidence, not from the neglect of the Whig leaders. It is
interesting, though, that the passage of time had not erased the
old charge against Steele of "imputed Wit," a fiction which had
originated during his open quarrel with Swift in 1713.

CONCLUSION

THIS ACCOUNT of Swift's later relations with Addison and Steele has necessarily been fragmentary. With the death of the Queen their lives took divergent paths, and the diversity of their fates made impossible a return to the amicable days of 1708, even had they been inclined to seek it. With Swift and Steele, at least, it is certain that the inclination would have been lacking. To some of us it may seem strange that these three "wits" should have sacrificed their friendship to politics. But in Queen Anne's England issues like the Tory Peace or the Protestant Succession were not to be taken lightly. Political fortune governed every phase of life, and it was seldom indeed that a writer could affect indifference. That a conflict of political loyalties should have destroyed Swift's friendship with two of his major contemporaries is regrettable, perhaps, but it is not surprising.

One cannot single out a specific point of conflict as the explanation for their private quarrel. When in 1710 Swift began to serve as the propagandist for the Tory ministry, his friendship with all the Whig wits was effectually at an end. His open break with Steele in 1713 over such issues as the authorship of the

Examiner or his share in the government's attack on Marlborough was simply the surface manifestation of a personal feud
which had been growing increasingly bitter for over two years.
But it can be said, I think, that their estrangement was the result
of the basic opposition of their interests. Addison and Steele
were primarily men of affairs, place-seekers committed to a particular set of principles and political leaders. Swift was first of all
a clergyman, loyal to his Church and to that "party" which he
felt would best secure the Establishment. The distinction is clear
even in the period of his closest friendship with the Whig
writers, during his residence in England in 1707–09. While
Addison and Steele were seeking advancement as Whig officeholders, Swift was writing against the ecclesiastical policies of the
Junto. His alignment with the Harley ministry did not seem to
him a betrayal of his "old Whig" political principles. But to
Addison and Steele, who were "new Whig" supporters of the
Junto and who thought in terms of practical politics as well as
general ideals, his shift of allegiance seemed disloyal oppor-
tunism.

Swift's attempts to obtain patronage for Addison and Steele
after his "defection" were deeply resented and merely exacerbated
his relations with them. Yet throughout his later years he referred with a certain amount of pride to the period when as a
man of influence he had sought favors for the Whig literary
figures with whom he had been friends. In the *Letter to Mr.
Pope* (1720/21) he wrote of his attempts to intercede on their
behalf and to maintain friendships regardless of political differences:

> I remember it was in those times a usual subject of raillery towards
> me among the Ministers, that I never came to them without a
> Whig in my sleeve. . . . Besides, having never received more than
> one small favour, I was under no necessity of being a slave to
> men in power, but chose my friends by their personal merit,
> without examining how far their notions agreed with the politicks
> then in vogue. I frequently conversed with Mr. Addison, and the
> others I named (except Mr. Steel) during all my Lord Oxford's
> Ministry, and Mr. Addison's friendship to me continued inviolable,
> with as much kindness as when we used to meet at my Lord Som-
> mers or Hallifax, who were leaders of the opposite Party.[1]

This account, of course, is slightly distorted; the "curse of party" had not allowed for such a pleasant relationship with the Whig wits during Oxford's ministry, and Addison's friendship had hardly been "inviolable" in, say, 1711. But his efforts in those years to obtain favors for Addison, Steele, Congreve, Rowe, and Philips remained the aspect of his relations with that group which he chose to emphasize, forgetting, perhaps, that those very efforts had been among the irritants which had caused an estrangement.

The manner in which this personal quarrel gradually became a subject of public comment is a prime example of the vital interconnection of literature and politics in the period. When Swift and Steele emerged as champions in print of their respective causes, their private differences were exploited by the press of both sides, and their battle of pamphlets was seldom separated from its personal background. The battle itself was waged on less than equal terms, for Swift's satiric artistry made short work of Steele's rather maudlin sincerity. In their political writings, at least, the softness of the heart was no match for the hardness of the head. Ironically, too, the literary fruits of their early friendship were negligible compared to those of their later quarrel; *The Importance of the Guardian Considered* is one of Swift's most successful satires.

Only occasionally did the temperamental and intellectual differences between Swift and his Whig friends reach the surface of their quarrel. But these differences were striking enough to readers in the later eighteenth century. Addison's and Steele's leanings toward the benevolist view of man, their praise of the dignity of human nature, their disparagement of "levelling" satire all recommended them to that later age which deplored the satiric temper of Swift's mind. As in politics, so in moral and intellectual matters, Swift belonged to a more conservative tradition than did the authors of the *Spectator*. Addison did not live to read *Gulliver's Travels*, and Steele's comments, if he made any, have not survived; but it is difficult to believe that these "polite and fashionable moralists" would have found it very much to their taste.

NOTES AND INDEX

ABBREVIATIONS

BOOKS:

Ball	*The Correspondence of Jonathan Swift, D. D.,* ed. F. Elrington Ball (London: G. Bell, 1910–14).
Correspondence	*The Correspondence of Richard Steele,* ed. Rae Blanchard (Oxford: Clarendon Press, 1941).
Letters	*The Letters of Joseph Addison,* ed. Walter Graham (Oxford: Clarendon Press, 1941).
Journal	*The Journal to Stella,* ed. Harold Williams (Oxford: Clarendon Press, 1948).
Prose Works	*The Prose Works of Jonathan Swift,* ed. Herbert Davis (Oxford: Basil Blackwell, 1939–).

PERIODICALS:

ELH	*ELH: A Journal of English Literary History*
HLQ	*Huntington Library Quarterly*
JHI	*Journal of the History of Ideas*
MLN	*Modern Language Notes*
MP	*Modern Philology*
PQ	*Philological Quarterly*
RES	*Review of English Studies*
SP	*Studies in Philology*

NOTES

INTRODUCTION: INTELLECTUAL DIFFERENCES

1. William Thackeray, *The English Humourists of the Eighteenth Century* (London: Smith, Elder, 1853), pp. 145–50.

2. *The Poems of Jonathan Swift,* ed. Harold Williams (Oxford: Clarendon Press, 1937), I, 88, 91.

3. See the discussion by Davis in *Prose Works,* II, x; and W. A. Eddy, "The Wits *vs.* John Partridge, Astrologer," *SP,* XXIX (1932), 36.

4. *Prose Works,* II, xxv–xxxii.

5. Ball, I, 182–3; III, 50–1; see also *The Wentworth Papers, 1705–1739,* ed. James J. Cartwright (London: Wyman, 1883), p. 85.

6. *Journal,* I, 254–5, 218; II, 482.

7. *The Spectator,* ed. George A. Aitken (London: John C. Nimmo, 1898), VI, 117. All references are to this edition.

8. See George R. Potter, "Swift and Natural Science," *PQ,* XX (1941), 97–118; and the review by Louis A. Landa, *PQ,* XXI (1942), 219–21.

9. Arthur E. Case, *Four Essays on Gulliver's Travels* (Princeton: Princeton University Press, 1945), p. 80.

10. *The Guardian,* ed. Alexander Chalmers (London, 1806), II, 136 (No. 107). All references are to this edition. For typical ridicule of Steele's "projecting" spirit, see the attack by Dennis in *The Critical Works of John Dennis,* ed. Edward N. Hooker (Baltimore: Johns Hopkins Press, 1943), II, 190.

11. *The Tatler,* ed. George A. Aitken (London: Duckworth, 1898–9), III, 359 (No. 183). All references are to this edition.

12. *Memoirs of the Life and Writings of Mr. William Whiston,* 2nd ed. (London, 1753), I, 257–8.

13. *The Englishman,* ed. Rae Blanchard (Oxford: Clarendon Press, 1955), p. 119. See the comment by Blanchard, pp. 425–6.

14. *Journal,* II, 527.

15. Ball, I, 324–5.

16. *Ibid.,* II, 186, 197; for other satires on Whiston by Arbuthnot, Gay, and Prior, see the account by Charles Kerby-Miller (ed.), *Memoirs of . . . Martinus Scriblerus* (New Haven: Yale University Press, 1950), pp. 334–5.

17. James Harris, *Miscellanies* (London, 1775–92), V, 538n; Edward Young, *Conjectures on Original Composition,* ed. Edith J. Morley (Manchester: The University Press, 1918), pp. 28, 43.

18. My discussion is greatly indebted to the essay by Louis Bredvold, "The Gloom of the Tory Satirists," in *Pope and His Contemporaries: Essays presented to George Sherburn,* ed. James L. Clifford and Louis A. Landa (Oxford: Clarendon Press, 1949), pp. 1–19.

19. R. S. Crane, "Suggestions Toward a Genealogy of the 'Man of Feeling,' " *ELH,* I (1934), 205–30; see also Martin C. Battestin, *The Moral Basis of Fielding's Art* (Middletown, Conn.: Wesleyan University Press, 1959), Chapter II.

20. See Anthony Earl of Shaftesbury, *Characteristics,* ed. J. M. Robertson (London: G. Richards, 1900), I, 248; Francis Hutcheson, *An Essay on the Nature and Conduct of the Passions and Affections* (London, 1756), pp. 13, 19; Joseph Butler, *Works,* ed. W. E. Gladstone (Oxford: Clarendon Press, 1896), II, 189; and Isaac Watts, *The Doctrine of the Passions* (London, 1732), p. 174.

21. For examples of this view, see Charles Hickman, *Fourteen Sermons* (London, 1700), p. 25; Robert South, *Twelve Sermons*

Preached Upon Several Occasions (London, 1727), I, 61–3; Dennis, I, 260–1; and *Spectator* No. 408.

22. See the introduction by F. B. Kaye to Bernard Mandeville, *The Fable of the Bees* (Oxford: Clarendon Press, 1924), I, lxxix–lxxxvii.

23. Crane, p. 220.

24. James Arbuckle (ed.), *Hibernicus's Letters: or, A Philosophical Miscellany*, 2nd ed. (London, 1734), I, 108.

25. Rae Blanchard (ed.), *The Christian Hero* (London: Oxford University Press, 1932), pp. xiii–xvi.

26. *Richard Steele's Periodical Journalism*, ed. Rae Blanchard (Oxford: Clarendon Press, 1959), p. 3; *Spectator*, III, 294–5; *Tracts and Pamphlets by Richard Steele*, ed. Rae Blanchard (Baltimore: Johns Hopkins Press, 1944), p. 121.

27. Cited by Crane, p. 212.

28. Kaye, I, 52–3.

29. Arbuckle, I, 374.

30. *Spectator*, IV, 29 (No. 257); VI, 10–11 (No. 397); *Freeholder* No. 5 in *The Works of Joseph Addison*, ed. H. G. Bohn (London: Bohn, 1903), IV, 411–12; and *Guardian*, II, 452 (No. 166).

31. *Spectator*, II, 420–1 (No. 169); and III, 41–2 (No. 177).

32. Maynard Mack (ed.), *An Essay on Man*, Twickenham Edition, III, i (London: Methuen, 1950), xl.

33. James Brown, "Swift as Moralist," *PQ*, XXXIII (1954), 378–83.

34. *Prose Works*, IX, 158.

35. *Ibid.*, p. 244.

36. *Ibid.*, p. 232.

37. For a general account of Renaissance optimism, its relation to the doctrine of original sin, and the effect of Calvin, see Herschel Baker, *The Wars of Truth* (Cambridge, Mass.: Harvard University Press, 1952), pp. 30–32; see also Michael Macklem, *The Anatomy of the World* (Minneapolis: University of Minnesota Press, 1958), Part III.

38. Antoine Le Grand, *The Man Without Passions; or the Wise Stoic*, trans. G. R. (London, 1675), p. 117.

39. Lowde, sig. A4ᵥ; Timothy Nourse, *A Discourse Upon the Nature and Faculties of Man* (London, 1686), p. 109.

40. Crane, p. 220; his view is contested by Ernest Tuveson, "The Importance of Shaftesbury," *ELH*, XX (1953), 267–85.

41. William Wilberforce, *A Practical View of the Prevailing Religious System of Professed Christians* (Philadelphia, 1798), pp. 22–3.

42. John Taylor, *The Scripture-Doctrine of Original Sin* (London, 1740), p. 250.

43. On Taylor and his answerers, see R. N. Stromberg, *Religious Liberalism in Eighteenth-Century England* (London: Oxford University Press, 1954), p. 116.

44. *The Works of the Rev. John Wesley, A. M.* (London: Wesleyan Conference Office, 1872), IX, 223; T. O. Wedel, "On the Philosophical Background of *Gulliver's Travels*," *SP*, XXIII (1926), 434–50.

45. Isaac Watts, *The Ruin and Recovery of Mankind* (London, 1740), p. 328.

46. Matthew Tindal, *Christianity as old as the Creation* (London, 1730), p. 390; John Leland, *An Answer to a Book, Intituled Christianity as old as the Creation* (London, 1740), II, 402; John Balguy, *A Collection of Tracts Moral and Theological* (London, 1734), pp. 315–16.

47. Thomas Boston, *Human Nature in its Fourfold State*, 21st ed. (London, 1770), p. iii.

48. *The Philosophical Works of David Hume* (Edinburgh, 1826), III, 90. Cf. a letter to the *Spectator* by John Hughes praising the journal for asserting the dignity of human nature, but adding, "You cannot be insensible that this is a controverted doctrine" VII, 308 (No. 537).

49. See George Boas, *The Happy Beast in French Thought of the Seventeenth Century* (Baltimore: Johns Hopkins Press, 1933), p. 141.

50. Arbuckle, II, 145–6; see also II, 130, 397–9.

51. *Ibid.*, I, 414–15.

52. *Spectator*, VII, 309 (No. 537).

53. Ernest Tuveson, "Swift: The Dean as Satirist," *University of Toronto Quarterly*, XXII (1953), 368–75; Wedel, *op. cit.*; Roland M. Frye, "Swift's Yahoo and the Christian Symbols for Sin," *JHI*, XV (1954), 201–17; and Louis A. Landa, "Jonathan

Swift," *English Institute Essays, 1946* (New York: Columbia University Press, 1947), pp. 20–40.

54. *Tatler,* II, 263 (No. 87).

55. *Ibid.,* pp. 390–1 (No. 108); *Spectator,* IV, 347–8 (No. 317).

56. *Tatler,* IV, 234–7 (No. 242); *Spectator,* VI, 264 (No. 451); V, 184 (No. 355).

57. *Spectator,* I, 177 (No. 34); and IV, 52 (No. 262).

58. *Tatler,* II, 390 (No. 108).

59. *Spectator,* III, 200–201.

60. *Guardian,* II, 380.

61. *The Works of Joseph Addison,* ed. Bohn, V, 152.

CHAPTER 1: SWIFT IN ENGLAND, 1707–1709

1. *The Miscellaneous Works of Joseph Addison,* ed. A. C. Guthkelch (London: George Bell, 1914), II, 239.

2. Ball, I, 61, 67.

3. J. C. Beckett, *Protestant Dissent in Ireland, 1687–1780* (London: Faber and Faber, 1948), p. 46.

4. Ball, I, 69.

5. C. H. Firth, "Dean Swift and Ecclesiastical Preferment," *RES,* II (1926), 4.

6. Ball, I, 80n.

7. G. M. Trevelyan, *England under Queen Anne* (London: Longmans, Green, 1930–34), II, 328. For a somewhat different interpretation of these events, see Robert Walcott, *English Politics in the Early Eighteenth Century* (Oxford: Clarendon Press, 1956), pp. 147–53.

8. Ball, I, 76.

9. *Letters,* pp. 91–2.

10. Peter Smithers, *The Life of Joseph Addison* (Oxford: Clarendon Press, 1954), p. 139.

11. As quoted in W. A. Eddy, "The Wits *vs.* John Partridge, Astrologer," p. 36. The discussion by Davis is in *Prose Works,* II, x.

12. *Tatler,* I, 8.

13. Ball, I, 100, 109.

14. F. Elrington Ball, *Swift's Verse* (London: Murray, 1929), p. 63.

15. Ball, I, 106.

16. Historical Manuscripts Commission, *Report on the Manuscripts of the Marquess of Downshire*, I, pt. 2, 861; Ball, I, 113; *Defoe's Review,* ed. Arthur W. Secord for the Facsimile Text Society (New York: Columbia University Press, 1938), V, 366, 371–2.

17. Ball, I, 83–4, 86–8.

18. Louis A. Landa, *Swift and the Church of Ireland* (Oxford: Clarendon Press, 1954), p. 56.

19. Ball, I, 105.

20. *Ibid.,* p. 111.

21. *Prose Works,* VIII, 122.

22. See the textual notes in *Prose Works,* II, 275, 277, 278, 281.

23. Irvin Ehrenpreis, "The Date of Swift's 'Sentiments,' " *RES,* n. s. III (1952), 272–4.

24. *Prose Works,* II, 25.

25. See J. C. Beckett, "Swift as an Ecclesiastical Statesman," *Essays in British and Irish History in Honour of James Eadie Todd,* ed. H. A. Cronne *et al.* (London: Frederick Muller, 1949), pp. 137–41.

26. *Prose Works,* II, xix; and see the note by Louis A. Landa in his edition of *Gulliver's Travels and Other Writings* (Boston: Houghton Mifflin, 1960), p. 538.

27. *Prose Works,* II, 2.

28. See Calhoun Winton, "Richard Steele: The Political Writer," unpublished doctoral diss. (Princeton University, 1955), p. 21.

29. Ball, I, 120–21.

30. *Ibid.,* pp. 126–7.

31. As quoted in Beckett, *Protestant Dissent,* p. 47.

32. *The Observator,* VII, No. 82 (Nov. 27, 1708).

33. *The Wentworth Papers,* p. 68.

34. Ball, I, 123, 124 and note, 127.

35. *The Observator,* VII, No. 77 (Nov. 10, 1708).

36. *Ibid.,* No. 79 (Nov. 17, 1708).

37. Ball, I, 128.

38. The use of the fictional letter for political pamphlets was common enough, but it is possible that Swift's choice of the form was influenced by the appearance on November 17 of *A Letter from a Gentleman in Scotland, to his Friend in England, Against the Sacramental Test*. This tract was praised in the *Observator* as a "farther Whet to the Malice of those *Irish* Clergy-men" VII, Nos. 79, 81 (Nov. 17, Nov. 24, 1708).

39. *Prose Works*, II, 284.

40. Quoted by Davis, *Prose Works*, II, xxxix.

41. *The Wentworth Papers*, p. 75.

42. Ball, I, 149; Landa, *Swift and the Church of Ireland*, pp. 58–9; and see also Swift's later account of this incident in his *Memoirs, Prose Works*, VIII, 121.

43. *Tatler*, I, 49.

44. *Prose Works*, II, 50.

45. W. B. Ewald, *The Masks of Jonathan Swift* (Cambridge, Mass.: Harvard University Press, 1954), pp. 43–7; see Maurice Quinlan, "Swift's *Project* . . . ," *PMLA*, LXXI (1956), 201–12.

46. Thomas Sheridan, *The Life of the Rev. Dr. Jonathan Swift*, 2nd ed. (London, 1787), p. 50.

47. *Prose Works*, II, xx–xxi.

48. *Ibid.*, p. 61.

49. *Ibid.*, p. 62.

50. See Quinlan, pp. 207–12.

51. *Tatler*, I, 45.

52. *Catalogue of Prints and Drawings in the British Museum*, Division I: Political and Personal Satires (London, 1870–1954), II, 293, No. 1512. On this issue of the *Tatler*, see Calhoun Winton, "Steele, The Junto and *The Tatler* No. 4," *MLN*, LXXII (1957), 178–82.

53. *Letters*, pp. 134–5.

CHAPTER 2: SWIFT'S CHANGE OF PARTIES, 1709–1710

1. *The Life and Posthumous Works of Arthur Maynwaring, Esq.*, ed. John Oldmixon (London, 1715), p. 200.

2. *Prose Works*, IX, 30.

3. *Letters*, p. 149.

4. *Ibid.*, pp. 134–83, *passim;* Lewis A. Dralle, "Kingdom in Reversion: The Irish Viceroyalty of the Earl of Wharton, 1708–1710," *HLQ,* XV (1951–2), 401–17.

5. Ball, I, 166.

6. For a detailed account of Steele's share in this dispute, see Winton, "Richard Steele: The Political Writer," pp. 61–80.

7. *Dictionary of National Biography,* XXXV, 413; *Journals of the House of Commons,* XVI, 242.

8. Trevelyan, III, 47–60.

9. *Tatler,* III, 90.

10. Smithers, p. 107; Dralle, p. 418.

11. *Prose Works,* II, 131.

12. *Journals of the House of Commons of the Kingdom of Ireland* (Dublin, 1782), III, 513.

13. See *The Poems of Jonathan Swift,* ed. Williams, III, 1089; and *Prose Works,* III, 239.

14. Ball, I, 181–2.

15. *The Prose Works of Jonathan Swift,* ed. Temple Scott (London: G. Bell, 1897–1908), XI, 129.

16. Trevelyan, III, 63–6.

17. *Tatler,* III, 390.

18. *Ibid.,* pp. 408–9.

19. *Journal,* I, 67.

20. *Essays Divine, Moral and Political* (London, 1714), pp. 42–3.

21. *The Examiners for the Year 1711* (London, 1712), p. 31.

22. *A Collection of Scarce and Valuable Tracts . . . ,* "Somers Tracts," ed. Walter Scott, 2nd ed. (London, 1809–15), XIII, 76.

23. *Letters,* p. 229.

24. Ball, I, 185.

25. *Ibid.,* pp. 167, 185.

26. *Ibid.,* p. 187.

27. *Tatler,* IV, 102.

28. Ball, I, 193–4; for a detailed account of his negotiations about the First Fruits, see Landa, *Swift and the Church of Ireland,* pp. 60–7.

29. *Journal,* I, 13, 15.

30. *Ibid.,* p. 55.

31. *Prose Works,* VIII, 123.

32. See Robert W. Babcock, "Swift's Conversion to the Tory Party," in *Essays and Studies in English and Comparative Literature,* University of Michigan Publications: Language and Literature, VIII (Ann Arbor, 1932), 133–49; and Case, *Four Essays on Gulliver's Travels,* pp. 107–9.

33. *Prose Works,* III, 111.

34. Walter Sichel, *Bolingbroke and His Times* (London: James Nisbet, 1901), I, 222.

35. See Bolingbroke, *A Dissertation upon Parties,* 10th ed. (London, 1775), pp. xxxv, 11; and Charles B. Realey, *The Early Opposition to Walpole,* Bull. of the University of Kansas Humanistic Studies, IV (Lawrence, Kans., 1931), 37–41. On the Junto as "new Whigs," see *The Letters of Daniel Defoe,* ed. G. H. Healey (Oxford: Clarendon Press, 1955), p. 390*n; Defoe's Review* [IX], 24, 26, 30; and *Eleven Opinions About Mr. H——y* (London, 1711), p. 35.

36. Charles Davenant, "The True Picture of a Modern Whig," in *The Political and Commercial Works,* ed. Sir Charles Whitworth (London, 1771), IV, 152; for an example of Harley's call for support by "old Whigs," see *Faults on both Sides* (London, 1710), p. 46.

37. As printed in *The Memoirs and Secret Negotiations of John Ker, of Kersland, Esq.* (London, 1726), Part III, p. 192. Swift detested Molesworth's attitude toward the Church, however; see *Prose Works,* IX, 58–9, and below, p. 140.

38. *Prose Works,* IX, 31–2.

39. *Ibid.,* p. 29.

40. Benjamin Gatton, *The Doctrine of Non-Resistance Stated and Vindicated* (London, 1711), sig. C3$_v$.

41. Ball, V, 65.

42. *Prose Works,* III, 111; VIII, 180.

43. Davenant, IV, 152.

44. *The Medleys for the Year 1711. To which are Prefix'd the Five Whig-Examiners,* 2nd ed. (London, 1714), pp. 36, 45.

45. Ball, I, 237.

46. *Correspondence,* p. 268.

47. *Ibid.,* p. 43 and note; see also John Loftis, *Steele at Drury Lane* (Berkeley: University of California Press, 1952), pp. 25–33.

48. Smithers, p. 197.

49. *Prose Works,* II, 24.

50. *Journal,* I, 13.

51. *Ibid.,* p. 52.

52. *Ibid.,* p. 68.

53. *Prose Works,* III, 3.

54. *Journal,* I, 97, 119, 127.

55. *Ibid.,* pp. 79–80.

56. *Tatler,* IV, 311. The paper which provoked this letter was No. 241 for October 24.

57. *Journal,* I, 111.

58. *Prose Works,* III, xiii–xvi.

59. *Ibid.,* pp. 20–21.

60. *Journal,* I, 145; *Correspondence,* p. 466n.

61. *Prose Works,* III, 26–7.

62. *Ibid.,* p. 178.

63. *Ibid.,* p. 179.

64. *Correspondence,* pp. 468–9 and note.

65. *Letters,* p. 253; and see Graham's comment, p. 100n.

66. *Prose Works,* III, 30–31.

67. *Journal,* I, 128–9.

68. See *Correspondence,* pp. 450–51n; and Winton, "Richard Steele: The Political Writer," pp. 19–21.

69. *Letters,* pp. 249–50.

70. *Prose Works,* IX, 29. See also *Journal,* II, 589–90.

71. *The Present State of Wit,* ed. D. F. Bond, The Augustan Reprint Society, Series One: *Essays on Wit* (Ann Arbor, 1947), p. 3.

72. *Journal,* I, 165.

CHAPTER 3: THE YEARS OF THE *SPECTATOR*

1. *Journal,* I, 164.

2. *Prose Works,* II, 250–51.

3. Robert C. Elliott, "Swift's 'Little' Harrison, Poet and Continuator of the *Tatler,*" *SP,* XLVI (1949), 552–3.

4. *Ibid.,* p. 553n. The statement from Harrison is given as quoted by Elliott.

5. *Prose Works,* III, 83–5.

6. *Ibid.,* p. 166.

7. *Ibid.*, II, xxxix.

8. *Medleys*, p. 265.

9. *Ibid.*, p. 248.

10. *Ibid.*, p. 415.

11. *Journal*, I, 218.

12. *Spectator*, I, 258.

13. *Journal*, I, 254–5.

14. *Ibid.*, II, 482.

15. *Ibid.*, I, 269.

16. For a detailed discussion of politics in the *Spectator,* see Winton, "Richard Steele: The Political Writer," pp. 135–87.

17. *Prose Works*, VI, 41.

18. Trevelyan, III, 192.

19. As quoted by Davis, *Prose Works*, VI, x.

20. *Journal*, I, 282.

21. *Letters and Correspondence . . . of The Right Honourable Henry St. John, Lord Visc. Bolingbroke,* ed. Gilbert Parke (London, 1798), I, 246; see Kerby-Miller, pp. 3–7; and R. J. Allen, *The Clubs of Augustan London* (Cambridge, Mass.: Harvard University Press, 1933), pp. 77–82.

22. *Tatler*, I, 3.

23. His *Tatlers* were sometimes adduced as evidence of his political apostasy: "Swift had been very conversant with the *Whigs,* had written several *Tatlers,* and some *Whig* Lampoons. . . ." Oldmixon, *Life of Maynwaring,* p. 200.

24. *Journal*, I, 300, 304.

25. *Spectator*, II, 210.

26. *Journal*, I, 320–21.

27. *The Poems of Jonathan Swift,* ed. Williams, I, 142.

28. *Journal*, II, 449.

29. John Nichols (ed.), *A Supplement to Dr. Swift's Works* (London, 1779), I, liii–liv.

30. *Journal*, II, 415–16.

31. *Prose Works*, VII, 28.

32. Winston Churchill, *Marlborough: His Life and Times* (New York: Scribner, 1933–38), VI, 495.

33. Abel Boyer, *The History of the Life and Reign of Queen Anne* (London, 1722), p. 524.

34. *The Wentworth Papers*, p. 212.

35. *The Works of Jonathan Swift*, ed. Sir Walter Scott, 2nd ed. (London: Bickers, 1883–84), V, 397.

36. *Spectator*, IV, 93.

37. *Prose Works*, IV, 80.

38. *Letters and Correspondence*, I, 365.

39. *Prose Works*, III, xxxii.

40. *Works*, ed. Sir Walter Scott, V, 374.

41. *Journal*, II, 452–3, 460.

42. *Tracts and Pamphlets*, p. 71.

43. *The Second Volume of the Examiners* (London, 1714), p. 29.

44. John Dennis, *Original Letters, Familiar, Moral, and Critical* (London, 1721), p. 300.

45. *Journal*, II, 472.

46. See the comment by Williams (ed.), *The Poems of Jonathan Swift*, I, 151–2.

47. *Ibid.*, p. 157.

48. *Journal*, II, 494.

49. See Vinton Dearing, "Jonathan Swift or William Wagstaffe?" *Harvard Library Bulletin*, VII (1953), 124–5.

50. For a list of his writings in support of Marlborough, see *Correspondence*, p. 466.

51. *Ibid.*, p. 71n.

52. Smithers, p. 232.

53. *Prose Works*, VI, xvii.

54. *Ibid.*, p. 123.

55. *The Letters of Thomas Burnet to George Duckett, 1712–1722*, ed. D. Nichol Smith (Oxford: Roxburghe Club, 1914), p. 5.

56. Burnet, *A Certain Information of a Certain Discourse* (London, 1712), pp. 43, 57–8.

57. Louis A. Landa (ed.), *Reflections on Dr. Swift's Letter to Harley* (1712) by John Oldmixon, and *The British Academy* (1712) by Arthur Mainwaring, The Augustan Reprint Society, Series Six: *Poetry and Language* (Ann Arbor, 1948), p. 3.

58. *Prose Works*, IV, 16. The material in brackets was omitted in all printed texts.

59. Ball, II, 39. Apparently Swift's original intention was to compliment Addison, not Steele.

60. Landa, p. 5.

61. For a detailed study of this affair, see John C. Stephens, Jr., "Steele and the Bishop of St. Asaph's Preface," *PMLA*, LXVII (1952), 1011–23.

62. As quoted by Stephens, p. 1022.

63. *Prose Works*, VI, 151.

64. *Ibid.*, p. 153.

65. *Ibid.*, p. 160.

66. Stephens, p. 1021.

67. *The Miscellaneous Works of Dr. William Wagstaffe* (London, 1726), pp. 257–8.

68. Pointed out by George Aitken, *The Life of Richard Steele* (Boston: Houghton Mifflin, 1889), I, 414.

69. Wagstaffe, p. 321.

70. *Journal*, II, 546.

71. *Correspondence*, p. 60n.

72. Laurence Hanson, *Government and the Press, 1695–1763* (London: Oxford University Press, 1936), pp. 11–12.

73. *Prose Works*, VI, 197–8; for other accounts, varying according to the party allegiance of the writer, see *Examiners*, II, 254–6; Burnet, *Letters to Duckett*, pp. 17–18; and Boyer, pp. 608–9.

74. Burnet, *Letters to Duckett*, pp. 255–6.

75. *Journal*, II, 589–90.

CHAPTER 4: THE PEACE, THE SUCCESSION, AND AFTER

1. *The Wentworth Papers*, p. 319.

2. *Berkeley and Percival*, ed. Benjamin Rand (Cambridge: Cambridge University Press, 1914), p. 108.

3. John Loftis, "Richard Steele's Censorium," *HLQ*, XIV (1951), 51–2.

4. *Berkeley and Percival*, p. 111.

5. *Journal*, II, 651.

6. *Ibid.*, p. 652.

7. Burnet, *Letters to Duckett*, pp. 38–9.

8. *The Third Volume of the Examiners* (London, 1714), p. 291.

9. *Guardian*, I, 319–20.

10. Ball, II, 26–7, 29–30.

11. See Loftis, *Steele at Drury Lane*, p. 31.

12. Ball, II, 34.

13. *Examiner*, IV, No. 2. All subsequent citations of the *Examiner* will be to the file of folio half-sheets at Yale University Library.

14. *Correspondence*, pp. 80–81.

15. *Guardian*, I, 377.

16. Ball, II, 37–8.

17. *Ibid.*, pp. 38–9.

18. Robert J. Allen, "William Oldisworth: 'the Author of *The Examiner*,'" *PQ*, XXVI (1947), 173.

19. See D. A. E. Harkness, "The Opposition to the Eighth and Ninth Articles of the Commercial Treaty of Utrecht," *Scottish Historical Review*, XXI (1924), 219–26.

20. Sir George Clark, *The Later Stuarts: 1660–1714* (Oxford: Clarendon Press, 1955), pp. 237–8; Trevelyan, III, 254–8.

21. *The Miscellaneous Works*, ed. Guthkelch, II, 271–2.

22. *Ibid.*, p. 270.

23. *Examiner*, IV, No. 17 (July 13, 1713).

24. *The Prose Works of Alexander Pope*, ed. Norman Ault (Oxford: Basil Blackwell, 1936), I, 182.

25. Winton gives a full discussion of Steele's writings about Dunkirk in "Richard Steele: The Political Writer," pp. 209–34.

26. *Examiner*, IV, No. 28 (August 24, 1713).

27. John R. Moore, "Defoe, Steele, and the Demolition of Dunkirk," *HLQ*, XIII (1950), 289.

28. *Examiner*, IV, No. 35 (October 2, 1713).

29. *Guardian*, II, 423, 470.

30. *Tracts and Pamphlets*, pp. 110, 119.

31. Winton, pp. 220–23.

32. *Letters*, p. 280.

33. Clark, p. 239.

34. Ball, II, 16.

35. *Examiner*, IV, No. 35.

36. *Englishman*, pp. 8–9, 406.

37. *Examiner*, IV, No. 38.

38. *Prose Works*, II, 67.

39. *Ibid.*, VIII, 5.

40. *Ibid.*, pp. 11, 14, 22.

41. *Ibid.*, pp. 17, 19.

42. *Englishman*, p. 63.

43. *Ibid.*, p. 70.

44. As printed in *Quadriennium Annae Postremum,* ed. Abel Boyer, 2nd ed. (London, 1718–20), VI, 255.

45. Wagstaffe, p. 129.

46. *Ibid.*, p. 141.

47. C. W. Dilke, *The Papers of a Critic,* ed. Sir Charles Wentworth Dilke (London: Murray, 1875), I, 369–82; Dearing, pp. 125–7.

48. *Englishman*, p. 235.

49. George Sherburn, *The Early Career of Alexander Pope* (Oxford: Clarendon Press, 1934), p. 64.

50. *Ibid.*, pp. 65–7.

51. The following account is a summary of that given by Kerby-Miller, pp. 14–29.

52. *The Correspondence of Alexander Pope,* ed. George Sherburn (Oxford: Clarendon Press, 1956), I, 229, 244.

53. Keith Feiling, *A History of the Tory Party, 1640–1714* (Oxford: Clarendon Press, 1924), p. 455. See H. N. Fieldhouse, "Bolingbroke's Share in the Jacobite Intrigue of 1710–14," *English Historical Review,* LII (1937), 443–59.

54. Clark, p. 242.

55. *Prose Works,* IV, 61, 80.

56. *Ibid.*, p. 57.

57. *Englishman*, pp. 415–16.

58. *Prose Works,* IV, 74–5.

59. *The Poems of Jonathan Swift,* ed. Williams, I, 180.

60. *Englishman*, pp. 435–36. Miss Blanchard tends to agree that Swift contributed the papers attacking Steele, but there is no evidence for this. By this time, personal abuse of Steele was a commonplace of Tory propaganda.

61. *Prose Works,* VIII, 193.

62. For a detailed discussion of this matter, see Professor Landa's introduction to the *Prose Works,* IV, xxv–xxviii.

63. See Robert J. Allen, "Steele and the Molesworth Family," *RES,* XII (1936), 449–54.

64. Landa, *loc. cit.*

65. Ball, II, 111.

66. *Tracts and Pamphlets,* pp. 176, 180.

67. Trevelyan, III, 277–9.

68. *The Letters of Daniel Defoe,* pp. 430–1.

69. *Englishman,* p. 228.

70. For a survey of Steele's campaign against Harley, see Calhoun Winton, "Steele and the Fall of Harley in 1714," *PQ,* XXXVII (1958), 440–7.

71. *Englishman,* p. 248.

72. *Prose Works,* VIII, 67.

73. *Works,* ed. Sir Walter Scott, IV, 272.

74. *The Letters of Daniel Defoe,* p. 430.

75. *Prose Works,* VIII, 32.

76. *Ibid.,* p. 45.

77. *Ibid.,* p. 48.

78. *Ibid.,* p. 200.

79. *Ibid.,* p. 66.

80. *The Wentworth Papers,* p. 361; *Prose Works,* VIII, xxi–xxii.

81. Smithers, p. 279.

82. *Tracts and Pamphlets,* p. 299.

83. *Ibid.,* p. 313.

84. *Remarks and Collections of Thomas Hearne,* ed. C. E. Doble *et al.* (Oxford: Clarendon Press, 1885–1921), IV, 325.

85. Aitken, II, 32.

86. *Richard Steele's Periodical Journalism 1714–1716,* ed. Rae Blanchard (Oxford: Clarendon Press, 1959), p. 61.

87. *Ibid.,* p. 155.

88. *Essays Divine, Moral and Political,* p. vii.

89. *Ibid.,* pp. vii–viii.

90. *Ibid.,* p. 41.

91. Burnet, *Letters to Duckett,* p. 305; Dilke, I, 368; Sir Henry Craik, *The Life of Jonathan Swift* (London: Murray, 1882), p. 300*n.*

92. Ball, II, 136.

93. *Ibid.,* pp. 154–5.

94. *Prose Works,* VIII, 88.

95. *Ibid.,* p. 92.

96. *Ibid.,* p. 93.

97. Ball, II, 137.

98. *Ibid.,* p. 214.

99. *Ibid.,* p. 224; *The Letters of Jonathan Swift to Charles Ford,* ed. D. Nichol Smith (Oxford: Clarendon Press, 1935), p. 50.

100. *Correspondence,* p. 304.

101. *The Wentworth Papers,* pp. 410–11.

102. Smedley, *An Hue and Cry after Dr. S—t* (London, 1714), pp. 13–14; Ball, II, 239–40. Similar to the *Hue and Cry* is *Dr. S—t's Real Diary* (1715), reprinted in Smedley's *Gulliveriana,* pp. 133 ff. It makes a great deal, too, of Swift's "Breach of Friendship" with Addison and Steele.

103. Ball, II, 233.

104. Landa, *Swift and the Church of Ireland,* pp. 78–81.

105. Ball, II, 286.

106. *Ibid.,* pp. 276–8, 421–4.

107. *Prose Works,* VIII, 134.

108. Smithers, p. 328.

109. *The Prose Works of Jonathan Swift,* ed. Temple Scott, X, 371–7; *The Works of . . . Addison,* ed. Bohn, IV, 469.

110. Ball, II, 394–5.

111. *Ibid.,* III, 3.

112. *Ibid.,* p. 16.

113. Smithers, p. 412.

114. Ball, III, 272; V, 466.

115. In the *Preface* to the *History of the Four Last Years of the Queen, Prose Works,* VII, xxxv. On the date of the *Preface,* see the introduction, p. xiii.

116. *The Poems of Jonathan Swift,* ed. Williams, II, 481–2.

CONCLUSION

1. *Prose Works,* IX, 29–30.

INDEX

A NOTE ON THE AUTHOR

BERTRAND A. GOLDGAR was born in Macon, Georgia, in 1927. He holds degrees from Vanderbilt University—B.A. *magna cum laude,* 1948; M.A., 1949—and from Princeton University—M.A., 1957; Ph.D., 1958. At present, Dr. Goldgar is an assistant professor of English at Lawrence College, Appleton, Wisconsin. THE CURSE OF PARTY is his first book.